THE MISSIONARY
and
THE DIVINER

Contending Theologies of Christian
and African Religions

Michael C. Kirwen

ORBIS BOOKS

Maryknoll, New York 10545

The Catholic Foreign Mission Society of America (Maryknoll) recruits and trains people for overseas missionary service. Through Orbis Books Maryknoll aims to foster the international dialogue that is essential to mission. The books published, however, reflect the opinions of their authors and are not meant to represent the official position of the society.

Manuscript Editor: Lisa McGaw

Library of Congress Cataloging-in-Publication Data

Kirwen, Michael C.
  The missionary and the diviner.

  1. Christianity and other religions—African.
2. Missions—Africa, Sub-Saharan. 3. Missions—
Theory. 4. Africa, Sub-Saharan—Religion.
I. Title.
BR128.A16K57 1987   261.2'96   87-14975
ISBN 0-88344-585-9
ISBN 0-88344-584-0 (pbk.)

To my parents
Maurice and Loretta
who shared life with me
in a world of colors

Contents

Foreword

With this book Fr. Michael C. Kirwen tackles what is perhaps one of the most central concerns for African theology today. What, from a Christian perspective, is the worth of the pre-Christian divine self-manifestation in Africa? Of what value are the traditional African religious signs and symbols, thought-forms and spirituality, rituals and personnel vis-à-vis these realities as they are in present-day Christianity in Africa and as they are indicated in the Christian gospel? Is there any useful relationship between the God of Jesus Christ and the God of traditional African religion?

As is well known, the answer missionary Christianity gave to these questions was generally negative. By and large, missionary evangelization in Africa frowned upon any and all expressions of traditional African religiosity and spirituality. In the main it officially continues to do so. It urges repudiation of these expressions as completely worthless or antithetical to Christian faith and belief. Several distinct responses are evident among the people who have been confronted with this proposition of missionary Christianity in sub-Saharan Africa.

There are certainly some African converts to Christianity who have been persuaded by this line of thought. They have tried to discard their prebaptismal world of religious belief and embrace the missionary Christian one in its entirety. But these are very few in number and the success to which their endeavor has led them is, if put to scrutiny, open to debate. The preponderance of empirical evidence shows, on the contrary, that among the people who have accepted baptism in black Africa, the great majority have neither wanted to abandon nor succeeded in abandoning completely many aspects of their traditional religious outlook. The severest Christian theological, doctrinal, and pastoral strictures have not deterred them from reverting to it whenever they thought it personally or socially necessary. Has this been a result of the hardness of heart of an essentially "pagan" people or a rather obvious sign of the Spirit?

The majority of black Africans have, of course, so far resisted the efforts of Christian proselytism altogether (though this is changing fast with the second category above gaining more and more numerical prominence). But those who have resisted the advances of missionary Christianity have objected to the overly exclusive doctrinal conditions proposed to them by the Christian evangelizers. Presumably, they have reasoned and concluded that their own religious universe makes as much sense to them where it matters as that advanced by the new teaching, or has something to offer to it.

Through the empirical (in contradistinction to the purely speculative) theological methodology he employs in this book, Fr. Kirwen demonstrates that this sensibility is substantially correct where several issues central to the Christian faith are concerned. He suggests that if Christian evangelization in Africa would let go of a certain jingoism as regards a particular set of symbols and language about God, evil, the Christian community and its ministers and ministries, and life beyond the grave, then it might be liberated from a dangerous myopia. It might be freed to appreciate the Spirit as it reveals God in traditional African religion "prior to, during, and after the time of Christian evangelization." At the very least, it might see the need and perhaps let develop a new pedagogy consonant with the universal self-revelation of God. It might take seriously the fact that, in Africa, traditional religion is a legitimate interlocutor of Christianity; they can work to fulfill each other and bring sub-Saharan Africa to a fuller awareness of the magnitude and magnanimity of God—the God of Jesus. This is not syncretism in its negative sense. Rather, it is the soul of a genuine African theology of incarnation that some African prelates called for after the Synod on Evangelization in 1974. In this book this call is taken seriously and it bears much fruit.

It is not without significance that it has taken someone of Fr. Kirwen's professional caliber and pastoral sensitivity to consider, in as thorough and empirical a manner as he does in this book, "the ethnocentrism of Western Christian theology" in relation to some of the most significant issues and questions arising from traditional African religiosity. Although there are many who can boast of being as conversant in missionary theology as Fr. Kirwen, few can claim to be as open, empathetic, and appreciative of the African people's deeply Christic religious values in as lucid a way as he is. Perhaps this book will serve as a much-needed compendium in the areas dealt with for all pastoral agents in sub-Saharan Africa.

Laurenti Magesa
Catholic Higher Institute of East Africa
Nairobi, Kenya

Acknowledgment

I wish to thank in a special way Professor Herbert Richardson, Sara Joan Talis, Laurenti Magesa, Mary Jo Leddy, and Jack Costello for their critical readings of the manuscript, their suggestions, and, above all, their encouragement.

A Note from the Author

When I first went to Africa in 1963, I was a young Maryknoll missionary fresh out of ten years of standard seminary training in Clark Summit, Pennsylvania, Chicago, Boston, and New York. Suddenly I found myself living at a mission station in an African farming area where several hundred small homesteads dotted the countryside. There was no electricity, no running water, no cars, no paved roads, no newspapers or telephones. It was a strange world to me. Neither my life at home nor education had prepared me to understand and live with this different way of life.

The closest thing I had experienced to this African situation was my childhood visits to the farms of my aunts and uncles who live in northern Ohio. They too had no electricity, running water, paved roads, etc. However, even without running water and electricity, my aunts and uncles still shared my "*cosmology*." As Catholics we all believed that God had created the heaven and the earth, and that Jesus was the Son of God who became man to save us from our sins; we didn't believe in ancestral spirits, witchcraft, bridewealth, or lineage ideology.

I soon found that in Africa the real differences were not that the people didn't have electricity, but that their way of thinking about the world was so strange to me. Their *cosmology* baffled and challenged me. To talk with my African friends, I first had to understand the way they thought about the world. I attempted to do this through language study, discussions, and conversations, like the ones this book describes between a Christian missionary and an African "diviner." Twenty-four years ago I was that missionary.

If a person loves someone from another society, sooner or later he or she will be influenced and changed by that relationship. And I have so loved my African friends that I admit they were converting me as much as I was converting them. Today, the conversations described in this book between the missionary and the diviner are conversations which go on inside me all the time. I have become *him* as well as me, and my home today is more *there* than here. "There," of course, is not just a place in Africa, but a different way of thinking about the world.

Before going directly into the conversations between the missionary and the diviner, let me prepare you a bit by outlining some of the key ideas of this African cosmology. These are ideas so basic and so self-evident that every African just assumes them. They are never argued. They are as natural as seeing things with one's eyes.

The African cosmology which emerges from the material of this book depicts the world as the creation of a unique God—there is no hint of polytheism. God is spirit and breath. God is completely apart from creation but at the same time intimately present to it through blessings of fertility, abundance, and life. There is no division of religious consciousness into a secular/sacred dichotomy. The world itself is a sacral entity, the primal creation. There is a cyclic continuum between the creator and the creatures.

At the time of creation, God created the sun and the moon as lesser beings to watch over and maintain the order of creation. These lesser beings are seen by some African friends to be mere manifestations of God and not special creations. Furthermore, some of these friends believe that there are also created spirits, called in the Zanaki language *Abasambwa*, as part of the order of creation. Others, however, believe that the *Abasambwa* are, in fact, spirits of dead ancestors who are no longer known.

In this East African cosmology, the creator God is the overseer of humanity and the world. However, the day-by-day management of this world is in the care of the sun and the moon together with the ancestors. The ancestors, in turn, are the wellspring of the life and health of the living, since life itself is recycled through procreation. From this perspective, immortality is in terms of a reincarnation in which newborn babies continue the life, reality, and, in some ways, the personality of the recently deceased after whom they have been named. When a person's name is lost, that person passes into the community of the dead unknown ancestors.

Because of the life-sharing and life-protecting role of the ancestors, it is necessary that they be contacted on a regular basis so as to know their wills and desires. This work is performed by the diviner-witch doctors and the elders of the clans—the religious leaders of the people. These leaders claim the power to be able to mediate the wills of the ancestors to the living in order to ensure that the primal order of creation is maintained.

The creation stories of these East African people teach that at one time God lived close to humankind and there was no disorder in the world. God's subsequent withdrawal was due to an accident and not due to a moral confrontation with humanity. The present world, therefore, is not seen as a broken world in need of a cosmic savior for restoration. Evil, on the other hand, even so-called cosmic evil such as storms, famine, and earthquakes, is always caused by immoral actions, whether personal or social, of living or dead creatures. These actions distort the primal order of the world and must be addressed in the here and now; there is no other world of final judgment, atonement, or justice. It is the role of the ancestors to maintain the order of creation by chastising and punishing the living for their evil deeds and by neutralizing the evil caused by other created spirits.

The sacral cosmology sketched above is somewhat typical of the cosmologies underlying many of the African religions south of the Sahara, whether in Southern, Central, West, or East Africa. Cosmologies of this type were the filters through which many of the Africans first began to hear and, more important, to interpret the Good News of Christianity. For example, when the missionaries in East Africa at the time of baptism renamed each person with the name of a Christian saint to be their guide and inspiration, the people understood those names in terms of a reincarnation of the Christian ancestors. They saw the ritual reception of a Christian name as a powerful new identity which they now possessed. Likewise, the Christian priests, ordained by the church to function in the name of Christ when doing the sacred rituals of baptism, evoked in the Africans' minds the charismatic rituals of the diviner-witch doctors consulting the ancestors when giving them their traditional names. Furthermore, the very Father-in-heaven prayed to at the time of baptism by the missionaries was none other than their own creator God, Kiteme, whom they had worshiped from the beginning of time. In this syncretistic way, the Christian and African religious traditions came into a living relation to each other.

Over the more than twenty years that I have lived in Africa as a missionary, I have been deeply affected and changed by my African friends. I have not been "converted" from my Christianity, but I have come to understand and live my religion differently and better through what I learned from them. Many of my African friends actually converted to Christianity; I would be ashamed if this had not also meant that they appreciated more fully their own African beliefs, so that they became better persons.

The real value of religious traditions meeting each other is that both can be enriched. In this book, I have tried to show what this enrichment has meant for the African and Christian traditions.

Introduction

The diviner-witch doctor had just sat down at a table in the parish hall. There were 120 adults present. All watched him with bated breath; many stood on benches to get a better look as he brought out his dice of old coins and seashells and tossed them out on a small piece of dried goatskin spread on the table. He began to shake a large gourd to wake up the spirits: *shuu, shuu, shuu* sounded the gourd. At the noise of the gourd, several women shrieked and ran out of the hall. Others were visibly nervous. As the diviner read his dice, he began prophesying about how the world would end in fire and destruction. Then he said: "This evening someone from my village will fall and be injured on the way home." The people from his village looked at each other in apprehension wondering who it might be.

The place was the Catholic Church at Ingri in the North Mara district of Tanzania. The year was 1983. This was my Christian community. The people had gathered at the mission for their monthly pastoral reflection day. Ninety-two of them had been installed as lay ministers of the Ingri Church. The topic for discussion was the relationship between traditional and Christian ways of healing. The people from Nyambogo village had thought it would be helpful to have a diviner show how healing takes place in the traditional religion. However, when the diviner began prophesying dangers on the road home, many began to have second thoughts about the wisdom of their plan. Some murmured: "Why did you bring that person here? What has he got to tell us? His rituals are dangerous." But nobody doubted the diviner's power or the cosmic vision underlying it. What he was doing and saying was immediately understood and respected by all. There were few in the crowd who had not benefited from the ministry of diviners even after they had been baptized into the Christian faith.

Diviners, lay ministers, Christians, traditionalists: How are these different religious roles integrated in the Christian churches of Africa south of the Sahara? What are the issues of maximum interest and importance that are being discussed and debated by the ordinary African peoples as they hear the gospel message for the first time? What does the process of interrelating African and Christian values and ideas say to Western and African theologians, Western and African Christians?

Africa south of the Sahara is, of course, a vast area containing over 400 million people with thousands of traditional cultures and languages. It is impossible, therefore, to speak of African cultures as if they were one entity. However, certain beliefs and customs are consistently found in most of the African traditional cultures: beliefs such as a monotheistic creator God, lineage ideology, and nominal reincarnation; customs such as polygyny, divination, widow inheritance, and witchcraft. Given this consistency, the temptation is to present as universal the findings and conclusions drawn from a limited sample of African cultures. I attempt to avoid this problem by clearly identifying the area and the people from which the material of this book is drawn. However, I feel that it is legitimate to present the insights drawn from this material as generally true for other African cultures that have similar religious and social customs; the greater the similarity of customs, the greater the possibility of sharing these same insights. Likewise, this material is intended to spark debate among African readers as to how closely their own traditional cultures mirror these same attitudes, values, and worldview.

The study of African religions and cultures is becoming a necessity for the pastoral agents of the mainline Christian churches* in Africa south of the Sahara. Since the early 1970s, these pastoral agents have had to deal with traditional religions in a way that was formerly deemed unnecessary or impossible. Formerly, African religions had either been ignored or dismissed by Christian missionaries as primitive, backward, and atavistic; they were said to be

---

* The mainline Christian churches are those that were started by the missionary movements out of Europe and North America. They include the Mennonite, Anglican, Lutheran, Seventh-Day Adventist, Catholic, and some Pentecostal churches.

dying out. Missionaries were sent into African countries without any training in traditional cultures and religions. The religious issues that led to head-on confrontation between Christian teachings and traditional practices were seen to be moral in nature rather than doctrinal. For example, the failure of Christians to be monogamous was seen as a moral weakness, a continuation of pagan marital practices; the validity of Western Christian theology regarding polygyny remained unquestioned.

However, despite a century of hostile Christian propaganda against the traditional African religions, some Christian leaders are now realizing that African religions have not been effectively suppressed. The values and traditions of the African religions have continued to thrive in both urban and rural settings through the ministry of the diviners and elders—the religious leaders, "priests," of the traditional religions—and through the traditional rituals, prayers, and ceremonies that fill the lives of ordinary Africans. The continuing vitality of African religions can be clearly seen in the extraordinary growth of the independent Christian churches. These churches freely interrelate Christian and African doctrines and practices in various combinations without being restricted and scrutinized by Western-trained church leaders who are unsympathetic to indigenization.

In the meantime, most missionaries and indigenous Christian leaders in the 1980s have yet to understand, in a systematic way, how traditional religions function in people's lives, nor do they know the traditional rituals and the official performers of those rituals. Most Christian leaders act, at least implicitly, as if baptism into the Christian religion entails a radical giving up of all former traditional religious ways, attitudes, customs, and values. A few, however, mainly those who have had long-term personal contacts with new Christians, realize that the traditional and Christian religions continue to exist side by side in the minds and the hearts of the new Christians. However, most of these insightful pastoral agents lack the training in African religions to deal with this syncretistic phenomenon on the level of cultural and ecclesial structures. The best response that they can manage, in terms of indigenization, is private decisions on pastoral problems that do not affect the larger structure of the church.

On occasions when it becomes obvious that the traditional religions are still a major force in the lives of the people, both Christian and non-Christian, the missionary and local church leaders have had to take a pastoral stand. For example, the outbreak of witchcraft in Sukumaland in Tanzania in 1980, which led to a government roundup of suspected witches, found Christians arguing for both sides of the issue. In response some Christian leaders, seeing this disunity, expressed dismay, saying that the social upheavals of the decade had led to a resurgence of "primitive" religion, especially its witchcraft dimension, which was now causing unnecessary conflicts in the lives of the faithful Christian people. Others deplored the failure of the methods of evangelization, saying that too little attention has been given to major issues that, like witchcraft, affect the lives of the Africans. As a result, they argued, the Christians were now being left prey to pagan forces in times of crises. A few others, both African and missionary, explained the witchcraft events culturally, saying that the mixing of Christian and African beliefs and practices—syncretism—is part and parcel of evangelization because people do not radically change their religion overnight. These latter see evangelization as a slow process in which values and attitudes are gradually reshaped, modified, challenged, and changed. Furthermore, they feel that these head-on conflicts and crises show church leaders how the Christian message is being understood and lived by ordinary Christians, and also identify the points of difference between Christianity and traditional religions. This, they say, challenges the missionary and local church leaders to be more skillful in attempting to communicate the Good News of Christianity to the local people in terms of their traditional religions.

This culturally inspired response to religious conflicts arises out of two sources. The first is the new knowledge of cultures and religions that is available to Christian theologians through the social sciences. The second, important for Catholics, is the mandate of Vatican Council II of the Catholic Church in 1965, which called for a dialogue with indigenous religions wherever Christianity is preached. The result of this cultural approach is that the very African religions that had been seen as obstacles to conversion are now being studied in order to understand the contemporary religious identity of the local people, and in order to see how Christianity can be incarnated into traditional ways and practices. African religions are now being viewed by some church leaders as major building blocks in the development of Christian communities.

In this culturally inspired approach, traditional religions are accepted as revelatory of God prior to, during, and after the time of Christian evangelization. This does not mean that there is an uncritical acceptance of each and every item of the traditional religions by Christians—no more than that there is an uncritical acceptance of each and every item of the Christian religion by Africans. Rather, evangelization is understood to take place in the interrelation of the local indigenous African theology and the particular local Christian theology taught by missionaries and indigenous leaders. Both of these theologies are limited by time and place; both contain only a partial understanding of the transcendent truths surrounding human existence. Both theologies look to each other for a greater fullness and fulfillment; both are calling men and women to go beyond the limited bonds of their cultural existence. At the same time Christianity contains the seeds of a universal hope of cosmic salvation that enables it to critique every cultural horizon as limited in order to strive for a truly universal human order. However, Christianity's very critique of cultures is also limited by its own peculiar cultural trappings.

Theologically the ongoing denial of the validity and power of African religions occurs because the theologies of the Christian leaders were constructed within the cultural framework of Western societies. Such theologies do not address, nor can they ever adequately address, African values, issues, and problems; their cultural roots are elsewhere. And even though such theologies are taught in African countries, they will remain forever foreign theologies, intelligible only to those who share a Western cultural perspective. A truly localized African Christian theology must address African issues and values and must be constructed within the conceptual framework of African languages, religions, and worldviews.

Pastorally the conservative, Western-designed structures and moral discipline enforced in most African Christian churches do not take into account, in any significant way, traditional African moral and religious values. Decisions for or against particular African customs are often made and enforced by Christian leaders without proper research, debate, and discussion. Western Christian theological opinion is often assumed as the norm by which one judges particular African issues, for example, the morality of memorial sacrifices to ancestors. If an individual pastor were to change the pastoral discipline and condone Christian participation in memorial sacrifices to ancestors, it would be inevitable that his decision would be challenged and changed if he were replaced by someone who did not accept his judgment on the morality of ancestral sacrifices. The end result would be unmitigated frustration on the part of the Christians. Because of this inevitable frustration, many pastors prefer to go along with the pastoral discipline of their church even though they judge this discipline to be not only inadequate but wrong.

Pedagogically African peoples, of necessity, will interpret the Christian proclamation of the gospel with all its Western cultural, philosophical, and linguistic elements in terms of their traditional religions. Thus, where Christianity seems to say the same thing as the traditional religions, for example, proclaiming the existence of a creator God, the Africans will respond that they already believed this before the preaching of Christianity. However, the Christian nuances about this creator God as triune and as Father will not be readily heard. Such nuances represent a major shift in religious consciousness for Africans. Shifts of this type come about only gradually with much debate, discussion, and dialogue—the very thing that the Christian churches that preach a prepackaged version of Christianity do not allow.

At the same time, if Western theologians could view their nuanced local Western theologies laid bare and skeletonized in foreign languages and cultural settings, they would be forced to reconsider how much of their teachings are philosophical and cultural rather than Christian. They might even begin to wonder, for example, if there would be a "trinitarian" model of the Godhead if Christianity had first taken root and flourished in the African world rather than the Greek world. Also, they might immediately realize how intolerable it would be to preach a Christian theology oriented to African issues and values to Western peoples, seeing that many issues debated in the African church—for example, polygyny, witchcraft, and lineal ideology—would be out of step with the needs, problems, and aspirations of non-Africans.

As a result of these theological, pastoral, and pedagogical conflicts, there has been very little progress in the Roman Catholic Church in Africa in indigenizing Christianity on the level of culture despite the mandate for indigenization given by Rome in 1965. In general this same lack of progress in developing a genuine African version of Christianity is also true of the mainline Protestant churches, and for the same reasons.

In response to these obstacles to indigenization, this book addresses the issue of evangelization in Africa from a theological, cultural, and linguistic perspective. It shows the complexity of transcultural theological communication in the concrete pastoral order. It points out the ethnocentrism of Western Christian theology when faced with certain African questions and issues. It reveals the vitality and power of the African traditional religions. It shows that both African and Christian religions are limited in their ability to resolve some of the major issues facing ordinary Africans. Furthermore, this work indicates that the traditional religious identity of most of the African peoples is relatively intact, and thus there is still a possibility of constructing an African Christianity that is self-designed on the level of culture. Also, it shows that a cultural approach to evangelization is absolutely essential if Christianity is to be truly indigenized in Africa south of the Sahara in the 1980s and 1990s.

The people discussed in this book are subsistence farmers living in the Mara district of northwest Tanzania among whom I have lived and worked since 1963. They live in grass-roofed villages of three hundred to five hundred families. Many are cattle raisers, and those who live close to Lake Victoria are also fishermen. The people in this district come from a rich variety of twelve distinct languages and cultures. This fact has tended to make the ordinary person open to novelty and has promoted a cultural sophistication rarely seen in the monolithic cultures of the world. Polygyny is widespread, ranging anywhere from 10 percent to 50 percent depending on the ethnic group.

These cultures have no written traditions. The wisdom of these peoples is passed from generation to generation by storytelling, songs, initiation rituals, celebrations of all types from birth to death, and through hours of listening to the elders discussing major life issues. In this milieu one of the fine arts of the people is skill in conversation. People are more than willing to sit for hours listening, talking, and discussing every aspect of life.

Christianity was first preached in the Mara district of Tanzania by a French community of Catholic missionaries, popularly called "White Fathers," at the turn of the century. The Catholic version of Christianity was quickly challenged by the Seventh-Day Adventists, the Anglicans, the Mennonites, and various Pentecostal churches. By the early 1970s all interested people had joined one or the other of the various Christian denominations. In 1972, for example, 85 percent of the Luo people claimed allegiance to some variety of Christianity. The neighboring Kuria, by way of contrast, had a 35 percent rate of Christian membership. The Kwaya people, to the south, had a rate of 47 percent. During the period of Christian evangelization, the traditional religious leaders of the people (diviners, elders, medicine men, healers, and herbalists) continued to perform their rituals and minister to the general population, including those who were now Christians.

From the beginning Christianity took a strong stand against the traditional African religions, especially the diviners and their rituals; divination was often equated with devil worship. The new Christians were to renounce all forms of divination, and any lapse was seen as a serious breach of faith on a par with practicing polygyny. All paraphernalia related to divination and the spirit world was often publicly burned as a condition for baptism. Likewise, severe sanctions were imposed by the churches on those who participated in divination after baptism. However, as with polygyny, many of the new African Christians ignored the churches' prohibitions on divination. They continued to seek out the services of the diviners whenever they were confronted with serious unjustified evil in their lives. In defense of a Catholic catechist who had hired a diviner to cure his bewitched wife, a Christian elder said: "He had no choice. This was a question of life and death. She would have died if he had refused to secure the services of a diviner." Christianity indeed prohibited divination, but it offered nothing as a replacement.

Diviners are the moral analysts, the charismatic leaders, the functionary priests of the traditional religions. Diviners know the African traditions regarding God, the ancestral spirits, the world, and life after death. In fact their very authority as religious leaders derives from traumatic, supernatural encounters with the spirit world that has turned them into mediums of the ancestral spirits. Diviners stand as salvific mediators between the living and the dead. And, since they are present to both realities, they are able to make known the desires, requests, and demands of the ancestral spirits.

Because of the diviners' ministry, the traditional African religions have continued to flourish. However, the role and function of the diviners are seen as real and understandable only because the people continue to believe in the underlying worldview and ideology of the traditional religions. As long as that belief is intact, the ministry of the diviners will be perceived as necessary and desirable. The continuing power and influence of the diviners in the African societies is a clear indication that Christianity, despite a full century of preaching the gospel and establishing church bureaucracies, has barely touched on the central beliefs, values, ideals, and visions rooted in the hearts of the African peoples.

The Christian position on the issues debated in this book is presented by me, an American Catholic missionary priest working in a rural Tanzanian parish as a pastoral agent from 1963 to 1970 without any skills or training in African religions. The Western Christian theology that I studied from 1959 to 1963, in preparation for overseas missionary work, was of the manualist type taught prior to, during, and after Vatican Council II of the Catholic Church. Accordingly, for many years my own theology was ethnocentric, and I preached Christianity accordingly. Only after my linguistic and anthropological study of the African reality in the 1970s did I begin to come to grips with the process of preaching Christianity in an indigenized way.

The Christian theology expressed in these conversations will be seen by many to be stereotyped, wooden, and without nuance. This is not accidental. This is the result of translating a local Western Christian theology that was created and developed in English, German, and French languages into African languages that have radically different symbolic systems and philosophical underpinnings. Moreover, most African and missionary church leaders are unable to preach and minister to Africans in an indigenized way because most have not been adequately trained in understanding African religions. As a result, this antiquated, Westernized version of Christianity is representative of what the African people are presently hearing through the preaching of the various pastoral agents: catechists, Sisters, laity, Brothers, priests, seminary professors, and bishops, whether missionary or indigenous, Catholic or mainline Protestant.

The diviner featured in the book is a composite figure. His words, judgments, and observations were drawn from live research sessions, which I—together with my students and African informants—conducted with a variety of African religious leaders over a ten-year period from 1974 to 1984. This primary research material is presently stored on tapes, mimeographed papers, and typed and handwritten papers and notes at the Maryknoll Language School in Musoma, Tanzania. The systematization of the African material was done in part with African informants and in part through group discussions with African leaders. In this process of systematization there was a certain amount of repetition and disjuncture of thought. This repetitious style was purposely kept to give the flavor of the African manner of argumentation.

The settings and scenes in the book are descriptions of actual places and events. Moreover, the conversations reported in this book are based on actual discussions; they are not contrived. Through the person of the diviner, they illustrate the people's genuine spirit of inquiry and ability to discuss systematically important matters affecting their lives. Discussions of these types go on for hours at weddings, funerals, feasts, and other celebrations—wherever people gather during leisure hours. All that is needed is someone to spark the conversation with a topic.

At the beginning of each chapter, I introduce the setting as a social scientist in order to facilitate a pastoral appreciation of the reality and urgency of this kind of debate and discussion in the African church. At times, also, I intervene in the conversation to help clarify various dimensions of African culture and to express my own changing understanding of the conflicts and issues being addressed.

The commentaries that I have appended to each chapter seek to delineate the important issues and dilemmas arising out of the conversations that are relevant to the Christians of the Western world. This kind of reflection represents a type of reverse mission in which traditional African theology challenges, judges, and enriches Western Christian theology.

The conversational style of this book was inspired by a Luo diviner from Nyambogo village in North Mara, Tanzania. He invited me, after a long discussion, to return with my tape recorder and camera so that he could teach me all the wisdom of his trade and ministry. The diviner felt that it was important that non-Africans understand, appreciate, and make use of all the traditional rituals and healing medicines of the African religious leaders. His hope was that I would share this wisdom with others.

1

God in the Absence of a Messiah

In the rural areas of Africa the missionaries spend a great deal of time traveling about the countryside visiting, preaching, and teaching. On one of my journeys I stopped, in the early afternoon, for a visit at the homestead of a Christian widow named Lucia Akech. I was unaware that her homestead was that of a famous diviner, Riana, and that Lucia had been living with him since the death of her husband. After the visit I found out that Riana was a well-known religious leader, a "priest" of the traditional religion, and was greatly respected and to some extent feared. People came to him from far and wide for divination as they sought to find out how and why evil had come into their lives. However, at that point in my missionary career, I was not at all knowledgeable about diviners or African customs and religion even though I had spent ten years after high school in a program designed by a missionary organization to prepare me for a lifetime of overseas missionary work.

I rode into Riana's homestead on my motorcycle and parked it near the house of one of his wives. My clothes signaled the traveling style that had become part of my missionary way of life: a windbreaker, a baseball-type hat, and heavy motorcycle boots. In a part of the world where there is no clerical garb, one learns how to dress for the journey through the bush. Riana's homestead consisted of six round, grass-roofed houses arranged in a circle with a corral in the middle.

Riana was as short and wiry as the graying hairs on the top of his head. Dressed in a tattered, short-sleeved shirt and black trousers, he sat on a three-legged stool in the shade of the grass-roofed veranda of his mud-and-wattle home. He had a distant, almost pensive look in his eyes. His gaze seemed to stretch the dark and leathery skin of his face.

I greeted the old man in his ethnic language, Kizanaki, as he strolled toward me with an extended hand. He shook my hand warmly, called for a wooden stool, and made me welcome. After several minutes of pleasantries in the ethnic language, the conversation switched to Kiswahili. I then inquired about Lucia. Riana answered in a low voice.

RIANA: Unfortunately Mzee Padri (Elder Priest), Lucia is not here. She went off to work in her gardens and has not yet returned. However, I am honored by your presence. You are the first padri to visit this homestead.

I have been waiting for a long time to have a chance to talk to a Christian missionary. A couple of times over the years I have met missionaries at funerals, but they seemed to be afraid of me as if I were some kind of strange person. Also, Lucia tells me that missionaries often preach against us diviners and our work, even saying that it is *Shetani* (Satan) or ancestor worship. Now, just why the missionaries are calling the ancestral spirits "Satan" is a mystery to me. I never heard of the word before they arrived.

However, the Christians still seek my help in times of trouble. Those who do not want to appear to be acting against Christian teachings come secretly; others, who do not seem to care, come openly. It has even been said that priests like yourself have been known to seek the advice of diviners in times of trouble. Personally I see my work as that of a healer, and I am not sure why you missionaries have been so negative toward that work. Usually I am able to help the Christian as much as the non-Christian. I could even be of service to you.

You know, Padri, for years I have heard a lot about Christianity; in fact, Lucia became a Christian long before my brother passed away. Lucia and I have often had long discussions about religion and the things she learns at church. Frankly, many of the things she talks about do not make much sense to me. She says, for example, that God is present in a piece of food, called "bread," and that we eat his body—an impossibility, since God is breath and spirit. She even speaks of a virgin giving birth to a human being who was, in fact, God—a contradiction to my way of thinking.

Padri, I have many questions about Christianity, and if you have time, I would like to talk about some of these things. I am especially interested in why missionaries have been so wary and suspicious of us diviners and our rituals. I have often wondered whether it is because you see us as rivals, since we are the leaders of the traditional religion. But are not missionaries also the diviner-witch doctors of the Christian religion? Or is it because you do not appreciate or understand the force of the traditional religion and the power of divination in the lives of the people, even those who call themselves Christians?

Long before Christianity arrived, Padri, there was a deep and profound religious faith woven into the ordinary activities of the people. This faith has sustained them through wars, famine, sickness, and death for thousands of years. Furthermore, since the beginning of time, our prophets and elders have struggled with and debated the major questions that surround human life. Are these the same questions asked by Christianity? And, if so, do the Christian answers to life's problems have any relevance for us, or are they confusing and unintelligible? I have often heard people say: "The missionaries speak our language but do not understand the meaning of our words." Do the answers of Christianity support and promote our traditional beliefs, or do they oppose and destroy them?

When I realized the situation into which I had stumbled, I was uneasy. I had had no idea that this was the homestead of a diviner. Diviners had always been presented to me as somewhat primitive, hostile, dangerous people involved in magical incantations and other ritual nonsense. I had never taken a course in or studied African religions even though I had been living and working in Africa for seven years as a pastoral agent in a rural parish. It was felt by most of my colleagues that diviners were to be ignored because they had little or nothing to offer the people and their influence was rapidly disappearing. However, as Riana talked I began to relax and enjoy the old man. Riana was an intriguing person. The thought crossed my mind that maybe Riana was really interested in becoming a Christian—a conversion that would demonstrate the power of the gospel. "Go ahead with your questions, Riana," I said. "I have plenty of time. I came to see Lucia, but since she is not here, it would be a good time to talk. I would really like to hear more about your religion, especially the worship you give to ancestors."

RIANA: Mzee, the respect given to ancestors, that you are calling worship, is difficult to understand unless you know the African creation stories. So let me start from the beginning. In our stories of creation, Kiteme, the high God, created all that exists at the same moment and, at the beginning, God lived very close to the people. The heavens were very low and, while people could not see God, they could see the heavens. Rain was abundant, food was plentiful, and death did not exist.

However, one day two men got into an argument. In anger the first one shot an arrow from his bow. The arrow hit the heavens, which were visible as a cloud. Immediately blood and water came forth from the cloud, and the heavens receded to where they are now. The rains began to fail, starvation entered, and death became the lot of humankind. It is believed that since then humankind has had no chance and will have no chance to live again close to God, Kiteme.

Another version of the story is that a young man out of curiosity (some say by accident) shot an arrow that hit the cloud. Blood flowed from the cloud and the sky moved away. The sun and the moon are now far away from humanity.

Stories related by other clans tell of a rope between heaven and earth, which enabled people to come down to the earth in the morning to farm and then to return to the heavens at night. Then, one day, the rope broke, or was cut by a trickster, and humankind was trapped on earth and unable to return to God. The Luo people tell of a chameleon who daily climbed a rope to heaven bringing to God a piece of meat from each and every sacrifice. However, one day a piece of meat fell into the dirt and the chameleon took the dirty piece of meat to God. God became angry and withdrew. Some even say that God is far away because of our sins—sins that are not against God but against each other.

As I heard Riana telling these African stories of creation and separation, they seemed primitive and simplistic. Only when he later on linked them to the story of Adam and Eve did I begin to realize that his stories of creation are similar to the Christian story, with the same level of insight and sophistication.

Riana interpreted these stories in terms of the primal separation of God and humanity.

RIANA: The break between humanity and God, Padri, is the fate of humankind. There was no test of the virtue of humanity. Humanity was separated from God by accident, and such is life. God and humanity cannot participate in one life. God is God. Humanity is humanity. However, our God is not remote from humanity. God created lesser deities, the sun, Iryoba, and the moon, Nyamhanga, to watch over and care for humanity (some say that these lesser deities are in fact only symbols and manifestations of the one God). The surety of the rising sun by day and the moon by night are the constant reminders of the warm and caring presence of Kiteme. In fact, one of our favorite names for God is "sun," the source of light and warmth. We pray:

Sun, yes, I am giving you this gift. Ah! Ah! Yaye! God, all-present one, our father. Shine on us in this land, blow softly, coolly, take away our sins, push them off into the sea.

Some say we worship the sun, but this is not true. The sun is given respect as a symbol of God. It is said that God climbed to the sun or is behind or on the sun. The Luo people say that the sun is the sign given by God in place of himself. The sun brings the breeze that dries the crops for the harvest. We pray to the sun to watch over us and to give blessings. In the morning God is greeted with the rising sun. A prayer is said: "Shine well on me that I might be blessed." Some people spit toward the rising sun in a gesture of reverence— the giving of their breath itself to the creator. The sun is like the eye of God moving back and forth. And in the evening as the sun sets, a prayer is again in order: "May you set well for me." Also, we pray to the new moon because it is seen as the source of life for the month.

One of our favorite images of God is that of a creeping vine, which is everywhere, spread out over all things. My father once said that there is no need to pray out loud like the Christians with many words and singing. It is sufficient just to sit quietly and acknowledge with awe the ever present blessings of Kiteme: family, crops, and cattle. God therefore is the creator of all creatures. God lives by God's own power. God is everywhere. God is good. God is the one who blesses humankind with children, abundant food, cattle, wives. All wealth comes from God. God is not a human being. God does not eat food. God is different from all creation. God is God.

Some say that God also created spirits called *Abasambwa*. Others, however, say that the *Abasambwa* are in fact the spirits of the forgotten ancestors. These spirits are seen as potentially dangerous to humankind precisely because they are unknown and cannot be appealed to for help or release. These spirits are said to dwell near rock formations or streams or forests. One must be careful not to offend them for fear of retribution. They often trouble and tempt people. Unusual and strange occurrences are often attributed to them.

In times of trouble, famine, war, pestilence, or lack of rain, sacrifices of animals are made to the unseen spirits beseeching their help in controlling these forces of evil. These sacrifices are performed by the elders as representatives of the community. Sometimes they are directed to Iryoba and Nyamhanga, the sun and the moon, sometimes to the ancestors, and once in a while to God—Kiteme. These sacrifices are attempts to reunite humankind with their offended ancestors who are punishing them for their misdeeds. And why are these sacrifices not directed to Kiteme, the creator? Because the ancestors are the intercessors for humankind and, furthermore, how can Kiteme be pleased with human food? Kiteme is above and beyond such mundane matters. However, some say that Nyamhanga is in fact a symbol of the power of God, and Iryoba of the light of God, and while these deities have been humanized, it seems to be tacitly understood by the people that their worship is intended for Kiteme. They are more manifestations of Kiteme than special deities. The ancestors, of course, ate food while alive and are still seen as able to enjoy a banquet. A Luo calls on his ancestors to eat as he offers his sacrificial cow:

This is the cow we are placing in front of you, O you ancestors, Kagose, Onyando, Ojode—accept it, all of you—it is yours. Call all your brother elders to come and eat it with you all. Bless this land for us—take away all the evil that the people have done on this ground, together with all the evil charms placed by the hands of the enemies. Now you agree with the things we give you. We are offering it so that peace will return to the land, so that sorrow will end.

At the end of the sacrifice, confident that his petitions have been heard, he prays:

You who are everywhere, who have brought us to this country, our spirits have revived. We have already cried to you— you have already heard us. May each one here leave this sacrifice with good luck and return to his house with a blessing. All our ancestors—bless us—let this death go to the sea. We have already eaten this feast. Do not let death begin to come near us.

These prayers show the special relationship and continuity between the recently dead ancestors and living humanity. The ancestors are close to God or at least close to Iryoba and Nyamhanga, and that is why they are able to intercede for the living. Besides, they are still personally present to the living through their wives and husbands, their children and cattle.

These ancestors do not become gods; they become spirits, and as long as they are remembered, they live with humankind. However, when they pass from living memory they become unknown spirits called *Ebehwe* or *Jachien*. It is the fate of each and every person to become eventually an unknown spirit—the final state of human beings. This is why people who are blessed by God have abundant children. The children ensure that they are remembered far into the future and by this they continue to participate in human life.

The community of the recent dead have great power and influence in our lives. They ensure that the moral order is kept. Their spirits reside in the grandchildren who were named after them. They often return and live near the trees of sacrifice.

We also approach God through memorial sacrifices to our

grandparents. They are the ones who put us into this land. They are the elders and owners of the land. They are the ones who have the power to prevent or ward off sickness, famine, and death. Evil comes when we break our ties with the ancestors. We pray:

> You, our ancestors, drive away the evil thing that is destroying us. Our fathers, we are disappearing from earth. Help us. All good spirits of the land, eat this sacrifice, especially you who were named after the spirits of this household. All you people who have gone to your rest, may you bless this your homestead. Take away all evil things. Look here: you bring peace to children and their mothers together with the cattle and the gardens.

Often these ancestors are explicitly named in prayer together with God:

> God has saved her [sick child] together with this good spirit [ancestor] that watches over this household. Chase away the evil chills in this homestead. May we receive all blessings of livestock. May our gardens ripen well for us.

Humanity's saviors, therefore, are the ancestors who keep the traditional order intact and coherent. Humanity returns to life in and through descendants. As the generation of elders dies out, the newly born children take their names and power. Part of the personality of a newly born is that of an ancestor. So humankind lives consciously in the light and protection of those who give and share human life. Indeed, human behavior is measured in terms of ancestral wills and desires. It is important, therefore, that harmony be maintained with them. They are the guardians of life and happiness. Respect for them brings blessings and abundance. Ignoring them can only lead to bad luck, sickness, loss of wealth and status. Ancestors are reverenced long after they have passed away.

The burial rites of the Africans usually go on for days on end with ritual slaughter of cattle, dancing, and singing. Indeed, for certain peoples, such as the Luo, the funeral rite is the central rite of their culture. It was only after many years that I came to under-

stand how these rituals teach the ordinary person the ultimate meaning of life and how to respect and honor the ancestors—the source of human life. Riana in his summary of the meaning of human existence indicated why the ancestors are so important.

RIANA: Life, therefore, Padri, is cyclic. Persons come and go. Humanity arises out of the life of the ancestors and goes back into the community of the ancestors. And how do we know of life after physical death? Because the dead appear in dreams to the living to ask that children be named after them, or to request that a sacrifice be offered in their names to assuage their anger over the immorality of the living. How could they appear in dreams unless they were still alive and close to the living?

Humanity's world is a closed, limited world full of human things both good and bad, joyful and painful. Relations with the ancestors ward off the dangers from the evil spirits, the *Abasambwa*, and the perverted men and women called witches. The ancestors intercede for the living and keep them in abundance and peace. However, behind the ancestors stands the creator God, Kiteme, who is pleased with creation and watching over it. Humankind, in return, stands in awe at the great gift of creation and life.

As I listened to Riana intently, the thought crossed my mind that these discussions suggested a new and exciting way of evangelization—a way of reaching the people through the traditional religious leaders like Riana rather than through individuals. At that point, as is customary, one of Riana's wives brought cups and a small kettle of tea. A dish of sugar was placed between us. As we sipped tea I began to respond in terms of a local Christian theology of the North American church, which I had studied while working for a Master of Theology degree from 1959 to 1963. In these conversations I attempted to express this theology as clearly as possible in a foreign language as it was being taught by me and my colleagues. Unfortunately, some of these ideas are still being proclaimed as orthodox Christian teaching despite the call of Vatican Council II for indigenized preaching. These are the things that I said.

MISSIONARY: Riana, I find your teachings and vision of God attractive and life-giving. God has not been far away from your culture. How many centuries of wisdom must have been at work distilling this revelation of God to you and your people: subsistence farmers and cattle raisers. Surely this must be God revealing God's life and presence. As one of our great leaders, St. Paul, has said: "How deep and unfathomable are the ways of God."

There are many questions that I want to ask you, but I think it best that I tell you about our God, the God of Jesus Christ, the one and only, the creator of all, the God of our father Abraham—the man who first believed in this one true God.

When God created the first man and woman, Adam and Eve, there was order and harmony in the universe. God walked with them in a beautiful garden called "Paradise." They were naked and felt no shame. All was at peace. However, God wanted to see if Adam and Eve truly loved him, and he gave them a test, telling them that they could not eat of the fruit of a certain tree. Temptation overcame them, and they ate the fruit, for they thought that it would make them into gods. Immediately they realized that they were naked. They had sinned against God. They were driven from the garden. Pain, suffering, misery, and death entered into the world of humankind. But God told them that he would send a savior who would free them from the power of sin and restore them to the previous harmony. This savior was awaited for thousands of years by a tribe of people called Jews, the descendants of a man named Abraham, the first true believer. And it was from this tribe that the Savior was born.

The Savior did not come as a mighty king-warrior, which the Jewish people had expected. He came as a humble man, preaching justice, charity, kindness, and compassion for all—especially the poor and sinners. He called on each person in the freedom of his or her own spirit to make a decision for truth and goodness. He promised to all who believed in him everlasting life—a life of fullness and happiness in intimate friendship with his Father, the great creator God.

The Savior was born two thousand years ago of a virgin, named Mary, in a small village in the country of present-day Israel. He was named Jesus Christ—this is why we call ourselves Christians, that is, followers of Christ. The fact that his mother was a virgin indicated that Jesus was conceived by the power of God and not the seed of an earthly father. He was truly a gift of God. His mother's husband, Joseph, took the child as his own and raised him. Joseph was a carpenter and Jesus grew up in obscurity in the little town of Nazareth.

When Jesus reached the age of thirty, he began to proclaim to the people that he was the long-awaited Messiah, Savior. He was the one promised to the first parents of the human race, Adam and Eve, when they sinned and broke their covenant with God. He was the one who would restore the harmony between humankind and God. Indeed, he taught that he had been sent by God to proclaim the Good News of the forgiveness of sin and salvation for all who would believe in him. He taught the people to call God their Father. He preached that internal virtue and love for all other persons rather than external ritual is what pleases God. In short, he proclaimed that God was calling each and every person to be like God while on earth and to come and live with God in everlasting life after death. If a person did not believe in Jesus, repent of evil deeds, and be baptized into the community of the church, then there would be everlasting punishment after death. Unfortunately, many of the Jewish people did not believe in Jesus, especially when he called himself the Son of God. Even his friends betrayed him into the hands of the Jewish religious leaders. The Jewish leaders, in turn, falsely accused him of blaspheming God and delivered him to the Roman authorities who crucified him on a cross. He was thirty-three years old. His followers fled in confusion and dismay. He was buried.

However, on the third day after his death, when his friends came to pay their respects at his grave, they found that he was no longer in the grave. He had risen. He began to appear to his friends, alive but transformed. He gave them a mandate to preach his Good News about God the Father and salvation to the ends of the earth. After forty days, in the sight of some of his friends, he ascended into heaven to take his place at the right hand of the Father.

Very quickly Jesus' followers began to worship him as God: the Son of God who became a man to redeem humankind from their sins. This community of followers was given Jesus' own Spirit, which we call the Holy Spirit. And it is this Spirit that animates, directs, and guides the Christian community to this present time. It is this Spirit that has called me and other missionaries to Africa to proclaim the Good News of Jesus about God and salvation. Jesus' very death on the cross is now seen as a great symbol of his love for all. This is why we proclaim him as crucified and put crucifixes in our churches, and many Christians wear crucifixes around their necks.

The Christian God, therefore, as revealed by Jesus Christ has a plurality about itself. It is a Father, a Son, and a Spirit. Each one is totally God yet somehow distinct. The Godhead is a community. God, the creator of all, the immutable one, the source of life, the all-knowing, the all-present, the all-good and all-powerful one, is a community. And this God-community has been intimately involved in the affairs of humankind from the beginning of creation. In fact God is calling you and me to share in God's very life, to become godly, to become more than human beings, to become God's sons and daughters. This is the true and real destiny of humankind. There is no other destiny.

This, then, is the God of the Christians. This is the God, the Father of Jesus Christ, whom we worship and serve, a God of power and might but, more important, a God offering us personal friendship through Jesus Christ. This God is a loving, communal God. This God is closely involved in the daily activities of each and every person. Without God's sustaining presence, we would cease to exist. God is calling each one of us through Jesus Christ the Son to join his community of believers, his Christian church, in order that we might encourage one another, correct one another, help and love one another, and call others to repentance and faith. Our God wishes that all persons be saved and brought to everlasting life. Without God we are nothing; with God we shall live forever. There are no other gods.

RIANA: Padri, as I hear you talk about the nature of God, I realize that the problem of many gods is a Christian problem not an African problem. You, in fact, preach three gods: Father, Son, and Holy Spirit. I know you say they are one and the same, but how can this be possible? Why do you make divisions in God? Even in your explanation you preach inequality, for a father always exists before and gives birth to his son. Is not your explanation similar to our teaching about God creating lesser beings who are godlike and have God's powers but who are subject to God? Is this what you really want to say?

MISSIONARY: Riana, you have picked one of the Christian issues that is hard to explain even in my own language. I don't know how well I shall be able to answer you in Kiswahili. However, I shall try. Tell me if my words make any sense.

I glanced briefly at my watch, realizing that the diviner had touched on a point of Christian doctrine most difficult to explain even in English. I wondered if I could ever begin to answer his question adequately, especially since we were lacking a common theological language. Moreover, the very language of dialogue, Kiswahili, was not a good medium for theological dialogue because it was a second language for both of us. I even wished I had paid more attention to this point of Christian doctrine while studying in the seminary. However, in the seminary no one had ever talked about this doctrine in terms of transcultural communication. Indeed, not one of my theology professors had even seen the need to translate the Western symbols used to express Christianity into the symbols of another culture. Christianity was said to be transcultural on the level of symbols.

In this situation I felt as if I were being transported back in time to the early years of the church when the gospel was first preached to the Gentiles in Greek and, like St. Paul, I was continuing the struggle to express the Good News in a foreign language.

MISSIONARY: I agree, Riana, that it does sound as though the Christians believe in three gods. However, this belief that God is a community of persons developed gradually over a period of three hundred years as the Christian community pondered on the life, death, and revelation of Jesus Christ. There was a growing awareness that Christ was equal to God. Thus, if Christ was equal, then there had to be some kind of diversity in the Godhead. Jesus also talked about his Spirit as a person separate from himself and even promised to send his Spirit to protect and encourage the community of the believers. This diversity in the Godhead was seen as the new revelation of Jesus about the nature of God, something that had been hidden from the beginning of time. Within four hundred years after the death of Christ, the firm belief of the Christian church was that God is three completely equal persons. God is called a "triune" God.

But how do you explain this threeness in God? And, as you so rightly objected, how can something be one and many at the same time? When trying to teach this in the Luo language to people who were studying for baptism I tried to find the right word to express this reality. The only word available was *kido*, which refers to a person's character—the way one expresses oneself publicly. They say, for example, *kite ber* (he has a good character). Applied to God as triune, it means God has three characters (*keche adek*); God has three different ways of expressing self. But this does not really capture the meaning of trinity, for how can one express oneself in three different ways simultaneously? Nor does it mean that God is a being with a split personality, sometimes the Father, sometimes the Son, sometimes the Spirit. In a Luo catechism written by missionaries, the word *kego* (to split apart) was used to explain this mystery. Things like paths, rivers, and roads *kego*, that is, split apart. So God splits into three parts. But again, this does not really express what the Christians believe about the inner life of God. For a path, as it splits apart, creates distinct independent ways united only by a common source. We do not believe that there is a splitting apart in the Godhead. The three persons remain totally equal yet somehow distinct. I finally concluded that there was no direct way to translate this idea of a triune God into the Luo language.

The Christian vision of God, however, is that there is some kind of community within the Godhead itself, almost as if God is a lineage—God is not an unrelated being without inner communication, loving, and response. Our great teachers throughout the centuries have struggled in all kinds of languages to express this deeply felt belief in God as trinity. However, all have only been partially successful, because the reality of God's inner life remains greater than anything that can be said about it. Nevertheless, we are convinced and believe that Jesus revealed this message about the inner life of God. We stand in awe, thankful for this new understanding of the life of our great and loving creator.

Riana, if you are to appreciate the truth of Christianity, you will have to expand your vision of the great Kiteme and begin to understand and appreciate him anew in light of the revelation of Jesus Christ. God is both one and many. God is a community of life and loving, a divine *jamaa* (lineal family). This is our God, the God of Jesus Christ. There is no other God.

At the same time, Riana, you also seem to believe in many gods. You say that your God, Kiteme, is the one and only creator. You also say that he created two lesser gods, Iryoba and Nyamhanga, both of whom have his power. And when you pray and offer sacrifices, you offer them to these lesser gods and not to Kiteme. So it seems that even though you say your God is one and only, in fact, in your worship and prayers, you have many gods. You call upon these gods in times of trouble and sickness and it is to these gods that you direct your requests for divine assistance and succor. Kiteme, you say, is the first and the creator, but in practice Kiteme has given his power and force to lesser gods who intervene and order his creation. You really do not understand and worship one God.

RIANA: You must realize, Mzee Padri, that our tradition has always maintained that there is only one unique creator, Kiteme. There is no other God. There is no one else who approaches, is equal to, or shares Kiteme's powers. Kiteme is alone, without family, without sons, without a community, without a lineage. Kiteme is totally different and apart from humankind, apart from all creation. This is our unshakable belief. We are not people of many gods like the Hindu or like you Christians who say you have three totally equal gods. The fact that God is unique and different is what led God to create Nyamhanga, the moon, and Iryoba, the sun, as constant reminders to us of his divine presence and care. What could be a more consistent and faithful sign of God's presence than the rising of the morning sun? What could be a more powerful symbol of God than the moon on a dark night?

Indeed, it was out of Kiteme's kindness that these lesser beings were created to do God's work and show forth God's goodness toward humankind. Moreover, many of us do not see these lesser beings as gods at all but, rather, as beings who mediate the creator's power to us. The very fact that they are said to be created shows that they cannot be gods, and to call them such is to use the word in a special sense. They are like God's overseers, God's special workers who enable us to see, remember, and respond to God. When we sacrifice to Iryoba, it is Kiteme who is honored. (How could Kiteme eat food anyway?) When we beseech Nyamhanga, it is Kiteme who hears. Our God, who is so powerful and great, cannot be mixed up in our human endeavors any more than a person can participate in the life of a cow. And this is why we say that Kiteme retired after creating. This is how we protect and proclaim Kiteme's uniqueness. Kiteme is so real and so present that we cannot even imagine Kiteme. We can only acknowledge Kiteme's greatness and thank Kiteme for the great gift of creation.

Furthermore, Kiteme is so different from humanity that it is impossible for humanity to be joined with God in one life as you teach. How can God be part of his own creation? Do not your teachings about Jesus dilute the true nature of God by bringing God physically into the world of humanity? Are you trying to say that God was also a human being who was born, ate, slept, suffered, got sick, and died? But what is your point? What does this add to our understanding of God? And to interpret the cruel, inhuman death of Jesus as a sign of God's love makes a mockery of God. Indeed, Jesus' death on the cross reinforces our belief that evil is within the human community and that God has nothing to do with evil. Jesus' death could only be the result of the evil wills of other persons, wills that would not have had any power over God if Jesus were truly God.

No, my brother, your teachings about Jesus do not make sense. You are contradicting yourself. You are calling Jesus by two names that are opposed and cannot be joined together. It is like calling a person both a man and a woman at the same time or like calling a cow a chicken. Why don't you just describe him as a created being who has been given special powers by God to care for the human community, like our Iryoba and Nyamhanga? This I could understand and accept. Either Jesus is God or a human being. He cannot be both.

MISSIONARY: Riana, it is clear from what you have just said that you do understand the radical claim of the Christians that Jesus is God. Again, you have asked about a central mystery of the Christian faith that is difficult to appreciate fully or to explain. Moreover, this claim is so familiar to me that I have never adverted to how strange it must seem to a non-Christian such as yourself. From your point of view, it must seem to be totally illogical and impossible. However, this belief is tied in with the belief that God is triune and that it was only the "Son" who became man, that is, took on a human form and walked among us sharing in our human reality. The triune God did not become a human being; only Jesus became a human being. This is the way we explain the humanity of Jesus so that we don't depreciate the power and uniqueness of God.

In one of our sacred books written many years ago by people who had seen and heard Jesus, it is not at all clear who Jesus actually was. He identified himself as the Messiah, the anointed one of God. But he did not give any indication that he was God acting like a man. He appeared as a holy person dedicated to doing the work of Yahweh—the creator God of his Jewish religion. However, after his death his disciples began to ponder the things he had said and done and began to realize that he was more than a man, that he was God. But this was not immediately recognized by all.

There were many discussions for over four hundred years as to who Jesus really was. Some said that he was in fact God, the second person of the Trinity, who only appeared to be a man. Others said that he was only a man who enjoyed a special relationship to God. Others said that he was both God and man by nature, but only God by personality—the final decision of the leaders of the church at a meeting held over fifteen hundred years ago at a place called Chalcedon.

Lately, however, some of our best teachers are again discussing who Jesus is. Some are even speculating that Jesus was only a man who was so open to the power of God in his life that God raised him up from the grave and brought him to live with him and made him godly. Prior to the action of God divinizing Jesus Christ, they say, God the creator was like your Kiteme, alone, without lineage and inner communication.

Our belief, Riana, in a triune God developed out of our belief that Jesus, the Messiah, is somehow both God and a human being. However, when teaching the Luo people about these matters, one must use the words *kido* (character) and *dhano* (human being). We say that Jesus, even though he was God, changed himself into a human being (*nolokore dhano*), or he came to us as a human being (*obironwa ka dhano*), or he carried the character of a human being (*noting'o kit dhano*). In these phrases there is no emphasis that he is really a human as such. He merely appeared as a man and expressed himself with human characteristics. The Luo language does not have other words to describe more accurately the Christian belief that Jesus is truly God and human at the same time—a belief essential to the Christian faith.

We call ourselves "Christ-ians," followers of Jesus Christ, not "God-ians," followers of God, because we feel that with Christ we are in the presence of the fullness of God's love and concern for humankind. To call Jesus the sun or the moon, as you suggested, could be a starting point in explaining the role of Jesus in the great creation of Kiteme. In fact, Jesus was often referred to as the rising sun in the early church—but one would have to go beyond that description and make clear that this Jesus is God and has the total power of God. Jesus is not a Christian "Iryoba." Just as God is both one and many, so also is Jesus Christ both one and many. Thus, Riana, our firm belief is that Jesus Christ, the Messiah, who was born a human being, ultimately is God.

Because of this belief in Jesus as both human and divine, there is the Christian hope that humanity can also be divinized and live like God. I firmly believe that humanity is incomplete if it does not walk with God or live close to God. However, in your belief, humankind has no hope of being anything but humankind-living-apart-from-God. There is no savior calling humanity to return to what was the original relationship between God and humanity at the time of the creation.

If indeed humanity once lived close to God, then humanity has since been cheated and will be forever restless and unhappy. For happiness entails being as close as possible to the source of life—God the creator. Otherwise, why would you even have these stories of an original time when God and humanity were close together? The question would not be possible without the desire and the need created by God. So you see, Riana, in your religion humankind's potential will never be reached. Humanity is a wounded, lonely, unhappy, and incomplete creation of God, unable to rise above its human limitations. Destined for what? To become an unknown dangerous spirit longing for redemption, longing for someone to come and free it from its misery, from its human condition. Your lesser gods, the sun and the moon, give humanity their blessings, but these blessings eventually fail. Your cattle die or are butchered, your wives become barren and old. Your children become your parents as your health fails in sicknesses; you can no longer eat, you die and go to the land or realm of the spirits, the ancestors. These blessings of your gods are temporary and corruptible. Where is the never-failing blessing? Where is the God who will make you live forever? Where is the God who will break the cycle that traps humanity into a hopeless existence?

At this point in the discussion, Riana's first wife invited us into the grass-roofed house where a table had been set with stewed meat and stiff porridge. Hands were ceremonially washed. The wife said a Christian prayer over the food. We began to eat together out of a common bowl, using our fingers as utensils. Only the right hand was used. Several small children joined us. As is usual, little was spoken while we were eating.

After the meal we returned to the veranda and Riana began to answer my question.

RIANA: Mzee Padri, you fail to understand that we feel no inner desire to live like or with God, Kiteme. The hope to live once again close to God is foreign to our way of thinking. We have such a respect and image of God that we cannot conceive of living with or sharing in divine life and power. Do you want us also to become suns and moons like Iryoba and Nyamhanga? No, what God has given us is sufficient. We are only human, and we shall remain as such. God is indeed the God of humankind—but God is also God.

Moreover, the reason there is no need for a savior like Jesus is that humankind has retained the goodness given at creation. Humankind has never been lost. It has never desired to be more than what God created it to be. To live with God or like God is impossible. In fact your story of the God-man Jesus coming to save humankind strikes me as a dream. God could never become human any more than the sun could become the moon. Don't you see how poor your image of God is if you can make God into a human? Then God is no longer God. Maybe, as I said, Jesus should be thought of as a lesser God like Iryoba, the sun? It almost seems as if you had to invent this God-man in order to say that humankind and God can and do live together and share the same life. And then you find in the human heart a desire to participate in divine life. But is this not farfetched? Have any of your ancestors returned in dreams to prove the truth of this teaching? Has anyone else ever risen from the dead? Mzee, my brother, humankind is most truly itself when it accepts without question its human life and reality and gives to God, the creator, the respect, worship, and love that God alone deserves.

Furthermore, Mzee Padri, you seem to take it for granted that people, after death, can live like or with God. What evidence is there that your ancestors have become gods? Why would God be interested in changing us from human beings to gods? Are you not mixing two things that cannot be mixed, cannot be put together, cannot be related? The creator and creation will always remain separate. Otherwise there will be blurring of the distance between them, giving humanity the false hope or pride that it will be like gods—the very sin of your Adam and Eve.

Your teachings, therefore, about the afterlife are unbelievable. They seek to interpret humankind as something entirely different from the way our ancestors have known and understood themselves from the beginning of time. Humankind is born from the stream of life shared with and flowing from the ancestors; humanity lives, dies, returns to the ancestors, and is remembered by the living. That memory comes alive again in the form of a newly born infant who takes the ancestor's name. This is the final fate of humankind. There is no other explanation that makes sense to me.

MISSIONARY: Riana, I agree with you that humankind cannot live with or like God. Humanity is a mortal creation destined to be born and to die. There is no way to get out of this cyclical pattern. Your forefathers seemed to know this perfectly, as you have said. For them life looks back to its source, the ancestors, and the ancestors themselves reappear in the guise of newborn grandchildren.

For you, then, life is a revolving, never-ending circle under the protection of the great Kiteme. Now, this is about all people ever knew about the afterlife prior to the coming of Jesus Christ. So it comes as no surprise to me to find this teaching among your people. Even the Jewish people had a similar idea of a shadowy existence after death. Yet Jesus proclaimed that humankind's destiny is to live with his Father and that it is possible to live on after death in a personal immortality if one is faithful to his teachings. We believe that this is an essential part of Jesus's message to humanity. Indeed, many of the Luo and Zanaki people who have recently become Christians said clearly that this idea of living with God after death is one of the most attractive beliefs of Christianity. And the reason given by our great teachers as to why everlasting life is possible is that Jesus has opened up to humankind a new kind of life, namely, divine life. Jesus, they teach, became man so that human beings can become gods. So, Riana, humankind is not trapped in a cycle of death and rebirth. Humanity is destined to new, fuller, and richer life with God the creator. And this is possible because Jesus combines in himself both divinity and humanity. Jesus is the proto-type of all that God wills for humanity. And, as God has graced Jesus with everlasting fulfillment and life, so too God will grace you and me and all persons whether living, dead, or unborn, if we prove faithful to God's commandments.

The issue therefore, Riana, that seems to be at the root of our differences about the final state of humankind is whether or not humanity can share in the life of the divine lineal family. For the Christians, humanity was created to share in God's divine life, and the break with God was caused by human sin. In your stories it appears that God's closeness to humanity in the beginning was arbitrary and the break accidental. Humankind is separated from God by no fault of its own. In your vision humanity is a victim of fate. If your God is so good and powerful, why does God leave humanity to its fate? Why doesn't God return humanity to the original creation where all was in harmony and peace?

Your stories of creation also show God to be a capricious and erratic being easily offended and angered and unable to offer mercy. Even human parents would be more generous to their children. And why should a stray arrow or a trickster or a broken rope or a dirty piece of meat decide the fate of humanity forever and ever? Is God not loving? Does God no longer wish to live close to humankind the way God did at creation? Are these accidental events outside of God's control? Is God only partially the God for humanity?

RIANA: Padri, it must first be said that these African stories of creation show that humanity was created whole and good and never lost its innocence before God. Humanity has always totally accepted God's will. When God and humanity lived close together before the break, it was a gift of God, and, after the break, humanity in humility accepted its new situation, without anger or shame. God gives and takes as God desires. Humanity stands as a humble servant never wanting to offend or move against God. Humanity has always said "Yes" to whatever God wills.

Why, then, you may ask, has humanity been separated from God? Who can know and challenge the wisdom of the mighty one? Surely God is wiser and more understanding than anything the human spirit can conceive. And even to suggest that God is unable to control the events that led to the break with humankind is to misunderstand God's power and place in the cosmos. If God wishes again to live close to humanity, it shall happen.

In the meantime humanity remains as a faithful servant. We praise and worship God for the great gift of life, the great gift of creation. The seemingly accidental nature of humankind's break with God teaches so clearly God's uniqueness and humankind's creatureliness. Besides, does not your story of Adam and Eve show a capricious and erratic God who is easy to anger, who wants to tempt creation, who is ready to punish the whole of humankind because of one man's fault? And, indeed, why should the fate of humanity hinge on the bad will of one man, Adam? Is there that much difference between the fate of humankind being decided by a trickster, a stray arrow, or a broken rope, as by an evil human will? The results are the same: humanity no longer lives close to God. This condition, we believe, is part of the plan of creation, part of the divine wisdom. There is no other explanation or answer. However, if and when God, Kiteme, desires it, humanity will again live close to God.

The linking of the African and Christian creation stories made me realize that all of these creation stories are mythical in origin. However, at that time I did not understand the full implications of this insight, namely, that the creation stories of the Africans function as the "Old Testament" preparation for the gospel, and that the Good News of Christianity could only be heard and accepted by Africans in terms of the truths taught by these stories.

The tropical sun was sinking quickly as we finished talking. I stirred a bit in my chair with a relieved smile on my face. Riana also looked a bit relieved, as the intensity of the discussion had taken a great deal of energy from both of us. But he was happy to have had the time to talk openly and honestly with me, the foreigner who was preaching Christianity to his people.

"Riana," I said, "I have found this discussion very interesting. We must continue it in the future. Why don't you come and visit me at the mission? I can show you the church and many of our sacred books, vestments, and articles that we use to proclaim and celebrate our beliefs."

"I too have enjoyed this conversation," Riana replied. "I shall see if I can work out a visit to your home next week."

At that point a middle-aged man came out of one of the grass-roofed houses, approached Riana, and spoke in a strange click language. Riana responded in the same tongue.

"What language was that?" I asked as the man walked away. "That is a secret language for psychic healing," replied Riana. "That man has been disturbed by an ancestral spirit and has been staying with me while undergoing a cure."

"Very interesting," I replied, wondering what this all really meant. I made a mental note to ask Riana more about this when we talked again.

I then got up, shook hands with all, and, as I strolled toward my motorcycle, told Riana to be sure to greet Lucia for me. I put on my cap, started up the motor, and, with a wave, rode out of the homestead. It was 5:00 P.M.

COMMENTARY

It is clear from this conversation that there are no theological words in Kiswahili or Kijalou to explain clearly and precisely basic Christian doctrines to Riana. The very words used by the African Christians to express doctrines such as the Trinity seem to have a life of their own and are continually used in contexts in which they have no meaning. The words themselves become the doctrine rather than the keys unlocking the doctrine. Could the doctrine of the Trinity, therefore, be interpreted to mean merely that the Godhead is dynamic rather than static when expressed in the concepts of African religions and languages?

As a foreigner I was impressed by Riana's depth and comprehension of the difference between the creator and the creature. The creation stories of the Africans bespeak a revelation from God that deeply affects their way of accepting and living life. The revelation is as complete and comprehensive as that passed through the centuries by the Judeo-Christian tradition. But how did these people come to that wisdom? Does this kind of revelation, without historical records, tell theologians something about the nature of revelation itself? Is revelation anything more than the collective wisdom of a people passed down from generation to generation and shared either orally or through written works? If Jesus had been incarnated in an African culture, would these stories be the "Old Testament" creation stories in light of which Jesus' incarnation would be interpreted?

The absolute monotheism of Riana put me on the defensive as I realized that what I was saying about God as Trinity must have sounded to Riana like a belief in many gods. In numerous ways the Africans have a purer notion of the uniqueness and unity of God than the Christians do. Christians have tended to popularize God as either the old grandfather or the fierce judge. Perhaps the calling of God "Father" has contributed to this humanization of God. Furthermore, there are no sexist pronouns in the African languages that designate God as either male or female, whereas the Judeo-Christian tradition historically has labeled God as male. Does the introduction of "Christian" sexist language harm the religious sensitivity of the Africans regarding God as pure spirit? Is traditional African religion a better vehicle for teaching the unique nature of God than contemporary Christianity? Has Christianity distorted its own revelation regarding the spiritual nature of God?

The contradiction the diviner sees in the discussion about Jesus as both God and human points out the complexity and difficulty of teaching such a doctrine in a foreign language. Furthermore, given the contemporary debates in Western Christian theology about the nature and work of Jesus, it is very difficult to determine exactly how or what to express as the Christian tradition about Jesus. In an ecumenical class of twelve theological students at the Toronto School of Theology in 1985, there were eight distinct Christologies. The spectrum of Christologies went all the way from Jesus as the second person of the blessed Trinity who became man but without a human personality, to Jesus as a man who was so open to the power of God that he became or was made the Son of God. In light of this debate over Christology in the Western church, what must and should be preached to the Africans as the Christian tradition about Christ? In terms of Christian orthodoxy, whose theology is to be accepted as normative in this debate?

The discussion on the final state of humanity shows the extraordinary nature of the Christian claim that humanity will live like or with God. Again, the problem is not resolved in the discussion. Riana does not even see the need or the possibility of such a final state for humanity. For him there has never been a decisive rupture of the primal order of creation. The Christian doctrine of salvation, on the other hand, presupposes a fallen humanity, a humanity that has been judged guilty of cosmic, original sin. Without the doctrine of original sin, would there be any need for the incarnation? Can the Christian doctrine of salvation be expressed in terms of the sinless worldview of Riana or is the conviction of sin essential to the Christian doctrine of salvation?

The religious role of the ancestors is barely celebrated by contemporary Western Christianity. This is in stark contrast to the central role the ancestors play in traditional African religions. Some African theologians have even suggested that the idea of the Christian God is best described to Africans as that of the chief ancestor. The question raised here is what do African religions reveal to Western Christianity about the community of saints—that very community of which we shall all be a part the day of our deaths.

The philosophies, theologies, and languages of Riana and me are so far apart that most of this conversation is a mere description of our various viewpoints. Even now true dialogue, in which there is some assimilation of the other's ideas and positions, is very difficult in the developing African church because of these same linguistic, philosophical, and theological obstacles—obstacles that will not easily disappear. An African Christian theology is sorely needed that can mediate the conflicts with Western Christian theology and boldly express Christianity in African symbols, rituals, and ideas. Moreover, there is overwhelming evidence that this conflict of worldviews and languages is not peculiar to the Christian evangelization of the African peoples. It is the rule and reality of evangelization wherever two or more cultures are involved.

2

The Source of Evil:
Divinity or Humanity

*Several weeks later I traveled to a village close to that of Riana
for a monthly meeting and liturgy with the Christians of the village.
I was pleasantly surprised to see a small group of people waiting for
me as I rode up to the outstation chapel on my motorcycle. Usually
people waited until they heard the motorcycle before congregating.
The outstation had been started a number of years ago by one of
my confreres at a time when the people were scattered, living on
their own homesteads. The site had been selected because it was at
the junction of two major trails. At the time of villagization, when
all the people were required by the Tanzanian government to move
off their homesteads into villages, the chapel area was chosen as a
place for a new village. The chapel then became the largest building
in the middle of three hundred grass-roofed homes. The walls of
the building were originally mud-and-wattle construction but were
later rebuilt with fired bricks. The floor was dirt and the roof was
made of simple wooden trusses covered with tin sheeting. On each
side there were three small windows with wooden shutters that were
barely functional. The double doors and frame were badly in need
of repair as the termites had been feasting on them for years.*

*After greeting all, I sat down at a small wooden table to write in
the names of the babies who were being presented for baptism—
this was one of the important elements of these meetings. It was felt*

that baptizing babies in the village chapels, rather than at the central mission station, would emphasize the fact that the whole village community is responsible for the socialization of the children as Christians. As usual there were mothers who apparently had shown little evidence of Christian faith or practice but who wanted their babies baptized so they would have Christian names. These cases were discussed with the other Christians. Finally it was agreed that two of these women could have their babies baptized, because they had been faithful to their religious duties. The others were put on probation and were told that if they began to show definite signs of faith, their cases would be reviewed after several months. The basic problem was that many of these mothers were either second or third wives, or their husbands were Christians who had lapsed into polygyny—an irreconcilable offense.

It was mid-afternoon when the Mass and baptisms were finished and the congregation began to move away slowly. As usual the chairperson of the community invited me over to a local teahouse for a cup of tea and some bananas. As I entered the house, I saw Riana sipping a cup of tea. We both smiled warmly and each of us extended a hand in greeting.

The Christians who had walked over and those who lived nearby began to crowd together at the doors in expectation of seeing and hearing what might transpire between us. The news about our previous meeting had been spread by Riana's wives. It had become a topic of conversation in the various villages of the area. Some thought it was a good thing; others felt that it was a step backward. The respect and attention that I had given the diviner was a source of confusion to many Christians who had been thoroughly taught that the diviner was a dangerous person and a threat to their faith.

"Riana," I said, "what a happy surprise! It is so good to see you. I have thought a great deal about our previous discussion, and I have been hoping that we would have a chance to talk again. How have you been? When did you get here?"

More people began crowding into the building as Riana started talking.

RIANA: Mzee Padri, I have not been well; I've had a bad case of malaria, and it has left me weak and achy. I'm just starting to feel better.

However, when I heard that you were coming to this village today, I came over, hoping that we might have time to talk. I didn't want to go into the church for fear of disturbing the people at prayer. It would have caused some concern if I had entered and attended the services. Diviners usually don't do such things. Anyway, I would enjoy talking some more about our religions.

MISSIONARY: Riana, seeing that you have just got over a bout of malaria, maybe the problem of sickness and evil would be a good place to start. We see how sin, sickness, and death trouble everyone; no one escapes them. Even people like ourselves, religious leaders of the people, do not escape. But why? What is the cause of evil? Why should humankind suffer these things? How do you understand this dark and painful side of human existence?

RIANA: Padri, I agree that the presence of evil, sickness, and death is a constant threat to the security of all peoples. Everyone wants to know why evil has come into their lives, because there should be no evil. The world, as the great Kiteme created it, is moral, good, and rational. It was created without any evil in it, for it is impossible for Kiteme to do evil, permit evil, or be involved in any way in evil. Evil, therefore, cannot be found in any plan of God. God is beyond and above evil. God is the source of only blessings: life, fertility, happiness.

Where does evil come from? The only possibility is that it comes from Kiteme's creatures, namely, humankind both living and dead. Some, moreover, would also add the *Abasambwa*, the created dangerous spirits. However, it is not certain that the *Abasambwa* are a special creation; many believe, as I said before, that they are merely unknown ancestral spirits.

Evil, however, always arises within the context of the human community; it does not exist elsewhere. Evil is caused by the immorality of the living, and that immorality must be neutralized if the moral order is to be restored. This is why unjustifiable suffering triggers in people's minds the thought that there is some immorality at work, either their own personal evil deeds, or some violation of the social order that has made the ancestors angry, or the action of a perverted human being, whether a man or a woman, whom we call a witch, *mchawi*.

People come to me to find out what is causing their problems. It is my work to divine the cause of the evil, to figure out the source of the immorality that is provoking the problem. Once the immorality is identified, then the person can take steps to neutralize it. For example, in the case of witchcraft, evil can be warded off by a powerful charm, or in the case of offended ancestors by offering a sacrifice of atonement. Often it appears that the breaking of the clan rules, such as the improper burial of an elder or marriage between forbidden clans, provokes the ancestors into sending suffering—and even death—until the immorality is corrected.

Recently there was a young man who married a girl whom traditional custom counts as his close relative. To the local people this union was tantamount to incest. However, he defied the local custom and was married in a government ceremony—the government defines blood relationships differently. He was repeatedly warned by the local community that such a union was immoral and would have terrible consequences. But he persisted in his situation and continued to live with the girl, relying on the protection of the government. Formerly he would not have been allowed to live in such a union; the people would have taken the matter into their own hands. However, in the present situation, he defied the elders, despite the objections of his relatives, who feared the inevitable consequences that would sooner or later engulf him and them also. The people said: "He has killed the dog." This expression is in reference to a covenant ceremony in which a dog is split in two, and the parties walk between the halves, saying: "May what has happened to the dog happen to me if I break this covenant." He had broken the clan's marriage covenant.

Several months later, at night, during a domestic quarrel the man beat his wife to death. When her family came to claim the corpse, it was said that there were teeth marks all over her body as if he had bitten her to death. No one was surprised. It was an inevitable conclusion to their immorality. The ancestors did not stand by idly but sent them death as a punishment and as a warning to others. His family was disgraced. People laughed at them for their stupidity in allowing their brother to act so foolishly. The people derided his family, saying: "What kind of human beings are you that don't even know how to raise your children to respect the sacred marriage laws of the clan, that tempt the anger of the ancestors? Are you, in fact, a family of witches, perverted human beings, antihuman, perverse, eaters of human excrement?"

Even in my early years in Tanzania, I noticed that whenever witchcraft was mentioned, everybody would become extremely attentive. This should have been a clue to the importance of this phenomenon. It should have raised in my mind all kinds of questions about the way people understand evil and sin in their lives, but it didn't. In this situation, the people crowding in at the doors and windows responded to Riana by smiling nervously and nodding in agreement. All knew these stories. The background chatter ceased as Riana continued.

RIANA: Of course, Padri, it had to be witchcraft; no one in his right mind would act that way and bring down the fury of the ancestors. So, Mzee, all evil, past and present, has a personal cause. It does not happen by chance. Even things like famines and epidemics—all arise out of the immorality of the human community.

Do you remember the problem with cholera last year when forty people died in a nearby village, and everyone was afraid it would come here? Do you know how it was warded off? The heads of each household were called together and told to purify themselves of all evil thoughts and feelings, and to reconcile themselves with anyone with whom they were at enmity. Then, on a designated day, all the heads of the households gathered early in the morning at the Angasaro River, each bringing dirt swept from the floor of his house. This dirt was then mixed together and thrown into the river by a respected elder. As this was done the elder prayed:

> Let this evil thing leave this village. Let it go to the sea with all evil things. Our grandfathers, Onyango, Riang'anya, come and watch over us. If we have offended, do not be angry. Keep this terrible death away from this village. See, we are sending away all our evil to the sea. Let us be at peace and in harmony.

Even the Christians participated in this ritual, knowing that it was the only way to ward off that dreaded disease. The ancestors heard our prayers. Not one person died of cholera in this entire village.

To us Africans it seems so reasonable to see the ancestors as the guardians of the public order. After all, it is their life that we share, and they are the ones who are closest to the source of life, Kiteme the creator. They are the ones who have the power to fend off the evils that affect the whole community, evils such as sudden death, war, starvation, and epidemics such as cholera. They are the owners of the land, the source of life, and it is under their careful guidance that humankind strives to keep in step with the harmony and order of creation.

Also, there are perverted human beings, the witches, who consciously try to injure their neighbors because of jealousy, envy, hatred, and bad feelings. These people, in various ways, seek to destroy the life force of others through sickness, chronic illnesses, and even death. These people can appear to be normal but at night they change. They become everything that a human being should not be. They walk on their hands, they fly, they have familiar spirits such as owls, dogs, and hyenas. Other familiar spirits work in their fields making them prosper more than their neighbors. The witches roam about at night making noises in the community to frighten people. They make medicines and charms to injure others. And the important thing is that these witches are always known people, neighbors. Witchcraft does not work at a distance. It is always between those who know each other. Witchcraft does not strike at random. And this is why it is necessary for one who feels he or she is being bewitched to find out and expose the enemy, the witch, in order to neutralize him or her or at least get a more potent medicine to ward off the evil power.

Recently a young woman died in a neighboring village. She had been to the government hospital where her sickness was diagnosed as stomach cancer. She had also tried the local herbal remedies but to no avail. After her death, her brother sought to find out who had been responsible for giving her cancer. He was afraid that if the guilty one were left unchecked, it could lead to other deaths. A diviner indicted a man whose house faced on the house of the dead woman. The accused man, when first confronted, said that he was a Christian and did not even believe in witchcraft. He denied that he had anything to do with her death. However, to prove his innocence, he agreed to undergo a traditional ordeal. (In the ordeal, one slides down a rough piece of metal—the spring of a truck—with a bare bottom, and the person, if uncut, is judged innocent.) The accused man slid down the metal and was cut. At that point he confessed that he must have had some bad feelings toward the woman, since the ordeal had found him guilty of being a cause of the woman's death. He was warned by the villagers that, since it was the first time he had been involved in such evil behavior, he would be allowed to stay. However, if it happened again, he would be run out of the village together with his family, and violence, even death, would result. He apologized to all, paid a fine, and promised that this would not happen again.

As the onlookers were voicing their agreement with the interpretation of the story, a young girl brought a plate of biscuits and a steaming aluminum pot of African-style tea (the milk and tea are boiled together). Eight cups were filled on the table and, after stirring in some sugar, we began to sip the sweet brew with some of the elders. There was a mild murmur of conversation as the people discussed witchcraft while waiting for Riana to continue.

RIANA: The people, as you can see, Padri, are very sensitive to immorality. They sense its presence when anything is out of order, and they make a definite attempt to repair the evil before it gets out of control. A few years ago, the daughter of one of the Christians in the village ran off with a young man as his second wife. It was said that the couple had been special friends since grade school days. Her parents were very upset because they wanted her to be married in your church, which doesn't accept polygynous marriages. They were certain that there was some immoral behavior prompting her actions. She had been an obedient child and they felt strongly that she would not treat her family in such a way. Sure enough, on consultation with a diviner, the parents found that the boy had made a powerful love potion, which had changed the character of the girl. The parents were then strongly encouraged by their own clan to make a counteracting potion in order to return the girl to her senses. However, since they were Christians, they felt that such an action would be a denial of their beliefs, and they refused to comply even though their friends pointed out that most Christians find no problem with such activity—indeed, Padri, many Christians have come to me for help and advice in similar matters.

After a period of time, the parents, under intense pressure from their clan, went to the local missionary for help. He told them that he would talk to the girl to see if he could get her to change her mind. The missionary was skeptical that there was any love potion involved. However, when he finally got a chance to talk to the girl, he found her so disoriented and dreamy that he thought she might be on drugs. He told her to visit her father and do whatever her father wished. She replied that she had tried to go home several times, but as she approached the entrance to her father's homestead, some invisible force had stopped her and she could not continue. She then promised she would try again.

In the meantime the Christian father wanted to know what to do to overcome the immorality of the young man who was abusing his daughter. He wanted to know if it was all right, as a Christian, to pay to have a counteracting potion made to rescue his daughter. The missionary told him he should not do it. Finally, however, in desperation, the father did turn to the traditional way of resolving the conflict. In order to save face, he instructed a pagan relative to arrange to have a diviner make a powerful charm to counter the love potion. As a result the girl returned home. A short time later she married a young Christian man as a first and only wife. So you see, my brother, even in the matters of the heart and relationships, there is always an identifiable person who is responsible for any evil and, more important, a remedy to overcome the evil.

Last year, for example, when the rains failed, the elders of the people gathered at the Mirari River where they sacrificed a goat to the ancestors and prayed that the ancestors would look kindly upon them and give them rain. There was no doubt in their minds that this evil had happened because the ancestors were withholding their protecting power and punishing the living for their immorality. They prayed:

> You grandfathers—don't be angry. Our evils are many in the land where you have brought us. Forgive us. Take them away from us—bring peace and blessing. Give us rain. May all the children grow up, the cattle be fertile, the boys and girls be well—bless us all.

All went away from the sacrifice convinced that they had attained their purpose of appeasing the ancestors. And rain did come, enough to get a harvest sufficient to last until the next planting season.

In another case a child was bothered by a chronic illness that left her sick and feeble. Her parents tried all the local medicines but to no avail. Finally she was brought to me to see if I could discern the cause of her problem. While divining, I found that the grand-mother, after whom the child was named, was the one bringing the sickness. The grandmother wanted a sacrifice of a quail. She was stealing the child's soul, leaving her listless. The sacrifice would entice the grandmother to return the soul and leave the child in peace.

On the day of the sacrifice, in the presence of all the older women of the homestead, the father took the quail in his hands, held it aloft, pointing toward the place of the rising sun while praying:

> My grandmother, daughter of Buoch. Yes, I am holding for you a quail—it is a sacrifice I am making for you. Accept it so that this child given your name will have peace—will become well. Return her soul to her so that she may not be listless.

Another man, Onyango, had three wives. The paramount wife had disappeared on a journey to Kenya during a time of heavy rains. Some felt that she might have drowned while trying to cross a swollen river. Others felt that perhaps she had merely run off and was living somewhere in Kenya. However, nobody knew for sure. After a period of years, Onyango became impotent. He came to me to find out the cause of his condition. I consulted the ancestral spirits and informed him that it was the spirit of his dead first wife who was causing his problem. She was angry that he had not buried her according to the traditional rituals; she had never been properly waked. In response, Onyango began preparations to mourn her as if she had just died. The whole clan was notified and the var-ious ceremonies were begun to escort her soul properly to the land of the ancestors. A grave was dug, and a few of her things were buried in it. The relatives came from far and wide to mourn her. Several cows were sacrificed in her name to feed all the mourn-ers. When the burial rituals for a first wife were all properly done, and her spirit rested in peace, Onyango's impotency disap-peared.

Evil of all types, Padri, can be caused by one or more of the following: the involuntary breaking of the clan's laws, the evil deeds of the living, the evil deeds of the witches, or, as some believe, the hostile actions of created spirits. All evil, therefore, has an identifiable personal cause because the source of evil is immoral actions. At the same time God has no part in immorality. God is above and beyond the wicked deeds and failings of God's creatures. Accordingly, it is the ancestors who ensure the proper order of the world and call humankind to account for their wickedness through various punishments, as we have already seen. They are the sources of life for the living, the guardians of the moral order. Nothing is done that escapes their attention because nothing happens by chance.

The work of the diviners is to help people sort out the source of the evils that have come into their lives. It is our belief that there is always a personal cause, a treatment, and a prevention for every evil, no matter how widespread it might be—like famine, war, and epidemics. To say that God is somehow involved with evil would be to make God less than God. No, God is only good. Evil comes from the disorder in creation caused by people and spirits who act immorally.

By this time some of the enthusiasm of the crowd had waned and a number were going off, especially the women who were to prepare dinner for their families. The second pot of tea, which I had ordered, was carried in and the little serving girl again filled the cups. She made a slight curtsy when finished.

I thanked Riana for his explanation of the problem of evil. I realized that what Riana was saying made sense to all who stood around. I also began to wonder if I would be as successful in explaining the Christian view of evil. This is what I said.

MISSIONARY: Riana, in our story of the beginning of the world, we too say that what God created was good and beautiful, and there was no evil in the world. However, the first parents of the human race, Adam and Eve, turned against God and refused to obey the divine commandments. As a result, they were banished from the garden where they had walked with God and were left to struggle for themselves. Once they left the presence of God, all kinds of evil arose: sickness, famine, quarreling, and, finally, death—their first-born son, Abel, was killed by his brother, Cain. It was the sins of the first parents, therefore, that led humankind into this present world, which Christians see as hostile and temporary.

Since then, our teachers have struggled with the issue of how a good God could allow some of the unjustifiable suffering that we see around us daily, suffering that is not due to the human will, suffering that even ordinary good people would rectify if they had the power—for example, starvation of children. Yet somehow we feel that even evil does not escape the power of God. God is so present to humankind that God cannot ignore evil. But if God is all good, then there must be some explanation of how God can at least allow unjustified evil to run its course.

Even Jesus was hard pressed to explain evil when his disciples asked him whose sin had caused the blindness of a man born blind: that of the man himself or of his parents? Jesus' answer was that neither had sinned, but that the evil had been permitted so that the power of God could be manifested. With that response he cured the blind man.

If personal sin, therefore, is not the source of evils such as blindness, then what is the source? We say that there is a cosmic evil, an evil beyond the touch of the fallible will of human beings. This evil is built into nature and is manifested in problems like famine, lack of rain, children born defective, the untimely demise of a loved one, chronic illness, and death itself. Some of our teachers call this kind of evil "original sin," since they attribute it to the first sin of the parents of the human race that led humanity into this broken, imperfect world. Others, however, argue that cosmic evil points to the fact that the whole world is in a state of change; it is not permanent. Humankind itself is part of these changes, which at times are experienced as evil. Others have argued that these cosmic evils are, in fact, only apparent evils, because we do not fully understand God's plan of creation. The latter argue that there is no need at all to justify the goodness of God in terms of the problem of evil. The fact of creation, of life itself, completely confirms the total goodness, wisdom, and power of God. How-ever, such an answer is not very satisfying to people who are in turmoil over evil that has befallen them. Yet Christians have always proclaimed that God cannot will evil or be directly involved in evil.

But God must be at least responsible for the possibility of evil within creation because nothing can be outside the divine power and will. This possibility of evil is tied in with human freedom and responsibility.

The power and pervasiveness of evil in the world has led many other religions to posit two kinds of gods, a good god and an evil god: one the source of life, the other the source of death. And usually these two gods are in mortal combat. But Christianity has always rejected such a notion of God. Christians believe that there is only one supreme God; there is no one else who competes for God's power.

However, from the beginning Christianity has taught the existence of a created, nonhuman being, which has been called the "devil" or "Satan"—the word you referred to in our first meeting. In Swahili the devil is called *Shetani* (Satan), a word borrowed from English because there is no Swahili word that fits what the Christians call the devil. In the Luo language the early missionaries, unfortunately, translated the word for devil as *Jachien*—the shadow or the spirit of the dead. This has confused many Luo-speaking Christians as to the real nature of the devil, because the devil is not the shadow or spirit of a dead ancestor.

Christianity teaches that the devil is a created, nonhuman spirit that is totally dedicated to evil from its own free choice. This devil goes about seeking to destroy the peace and harmony of creation. At the same time Christians understand that even the devil is under the power of God. But why does God allow the devil to have influence over humanity? Why is the devil allowed to tempt humanity? These questions have troubled us from the beginning and continue to trouble us. At the same time, Christianity perceives a cosmic battle between Jesus, the ultimate source of salvation for humanity, and the devil. We believe, however, that this battle has already been won by Jesus. Jesus has broken the power of the devil and, if we follow Jesus, the devil cannot have any lasting power over us.

In our sacred book, the Bible, the devil is called the owner of the world, the prince of the powers of darkness, the evil one, the hater of God, the father of lies. As Christians, we see the power of the devil as a very real threat to our relationships with God and one another. Often people will blame tragic behavior or accidents on the power of the devil. There are even cases of people being possessed by the devil. These people, Riana, obtain relief only when the devil is exorcised by a Christian priest in a ritual that is much the same as the one you use in similar cases.

As I said these words about exorcism, my mind flashed back to a session I had once attended where some local Christians were exorcising a woman who, they said, was possessed by a spirit they were calling Satan. The woman was in a high state of agitation and it took four young men to hold her down. The leader of the exorcism kept demanding that the spirit speak and reveal its name. The rest of the people continued to pray and sing, calling on Jesus to help the woman. Finally, the spirit spoke through the woman in a high-pitched, strange voice. It admitted that it was the grandmother after whom the woman had been named. Once the spirit's identity was known, the leader seemed to have power over her and commanded her to leave the woman in peace. The spirit responded, saying: "Good-bye, I'm going." The woman then slipped into a deep, catatonic trance from which she was aroused only with difficulty.

Some of the people said: "You see, Padri, how difficult it is to drive out the devil the way Jesus did." I responded that it wasn't the devil at all that was involved; it was an ancestral spirit, and if it had been the devil of the Christian faith, it would not have been chased away with such ease.

However, I held back from telling Riana this story as I thought it might sidetrack us into discussing the phenomenon of exorcism. I continued with my explanation of evil.

MISSIONARY: Riana, our vision of the role of evil in the human community, as you can see, entails two distinct orders, the one human, the other cosmic. The human order, the evil actions of men and women, are seen as sources of evil much the way you have explained it. However, we add the dimension that the evil we do to one another affects God. God measures our fidelity, faith, and love by the way we treat our brothers and sisters. We cannot say that we love and serve God while there is evil in our hearts toward our neighbors. Our sacred book quotes Jesus as saying: "Whatsoever you do to the least of your brothers, that you do unto me."

Likewise, we firmly believe that Jesus gives each one of us the power to overcome personal evil through faith, hope, and love—gifts of the creator. We feel that without God's direct intervention in our lives, we would continue to go on sinning and doing evil without any control over our actions. We would be blinded by envy, jealousy, and hatred.

However, we also see that the very ability to do evil is a sign of the freedom that God has given to each person. This freedom is so real that one can make a final, tragic choice to reject God's love and goodness forever. This shows us how genuine God's offer of friendship is. God will not force love and service from us. God wants only our freely given allegiance.

Within this cosmic framework Christianity perceives two related but distinct worlds: the world as God originally created it when God walked with Adam and Eve in the garden and this present world of trial and turmoil—the result of the first parents' rejection of God. However, there is the Christian belief that the primal world order will be restored and returned to humanity when the course of creation reaches a point set by the creator. Then God will once again walk with humanity in the primal garden. There will be no evil in that place, no mourning, no sickness, and all will live in peace and harmony together with God. The image of this great harmony is expressed in the image of the lamb and the lion lying down together.

Often Christian people interpret suffering as a warning or punishment from God because of their sins. However, both the just and the unjust suffer. All humanity grows ill, weakens, and eventually dies. Cosmic evil is so widespread that one cannot honestly see it as punishment or warning from God. But still there is the desire to know why evil has come into one's life. And the final answer is that evil must somehow fit into the plan of God for the individuals involved. Otherwise, evil would be irrational, meaningless. Evil must have a meaning. I remember when I was a young boy, I served at a funeral Mass for an eighteen-year-old neighbor. He had been killed as a soldier while fighting the Japanese. Nobody, especially his mother, would accept his untimely death as meaningless. The priest at the funeral service consoled her by saying that she now had a saint in heaven praying for her and watching over her, and furthermore, it must have been part of God's plan that he die so young. Indeed, he mused, God must have called him when he was best prepared to die.

Death for Christians, Riana, is the end of life in this temporary world. One dies when God the creator calls, not before or after. Life is in God's hand and no one has any control over life. That is why suicides, murders, and even killings in wars, despite what the priest said to the soldier's mother, are a direct affront to the creator God. Likewise, the good and bad deeds that one does are taken to the afterlife where they will be given a final, eternal judgment. The people whose deeds are virtuous and loving will live with God and all the holy ancestors in peace and happiness forever in a place called "heaven"; those whose deeds are evil will live forever with the devil in misery and shame in a place of fire called "hell." The Luo Christian people sing the following song in church:

> When Jesus returns, there is going to be a judgment.
> Those who love good actions will feel happiness.
> Those who do not love good actions will be dismayed.

The final state of an individual is due to free choices that were made while the person was living. Individuals can choose to live in sin or in virtue. And even though it seems at times that an evil man or woman is not punished in this life, we believe that all evil will be judged and all virtue rewarded in God's own good time.

Riana, there are many more things that can be added to this discussion, but I think that I have covered the essentials so that you can get a sense of how a Christian deals with the problem of evil—a truly frustrating problem.

As I paused a young girl entered carrying a tray of food. The cups were removed from the table, and the table was set. Most of the people began to move out of the house to allow the guests to eat. Several of the older men stayed at the table; others left. Each seemed to know what was required socially.

Small aluminum dishes were placed in front of each person and baskets of stiff porridge were placed at each end of the table. Pieces of meat were spooned into the dishes from a pot, and the gravy from the stew was poured over the meat. The pot itself was then set in the center of the table. Hands were washed in a basin carried to each guest by a young girl who poured the water from a small tea kettle. She then said a Christian prayer over the food and welcomed all to eat. Stiff porridge was broken off from the common bowl, dipped into the gravy, and eaten. The conversation slackened as all ate heartily.

At the end of the meal, when the tea was again brought, people started to move back into the building and cups of tea were shared with all the newcomers, both men and women. When all were comfortable again, I began to question Riana about his theology of evil.

MISSIONARY: Riana, I have found your teachings about evil to be very challenging and interesting. It is obvious that these teachings are the product of generations of reflection on the meaning of evil. But there are some things you said that I do not entirely understand. First of all, you say that all evils, even what we Christians call cosmic evils, such as famine, epidemics, earthquakes, destructive storms, and lightning bolts, come from the immorality of created beings either human or spiritual. You also say that the ancestors have power to at least ward off those evils from the living, but God has nothing to do with evil. Yet where do the ancestors get their power over these evils? Surely you do not believe that they were able to manipulate cosmic evils when they were alive. Where are the living elders today who have such powers? What then is the source of ancestral power over cosmic evil? Is it their closeness to the creator, Kiteme, and is it really Kiteme's power that they apply? And if it is Kiteme's power, then how can you say that Kiteme is not involved in evil? Riana, humankind whether living or dead does not have the power or ability to manipulate evil within the world. God has to be the one who is ultimately in control of the universe and, therefore, God has to be involved in evil.

RIANA: It is obvious from your question, Padri, that you do not completely understand how our African religion attempts to work out the problem of evil. You fail to see that Kiteme turned over the care of this world to Iryoba and Nyamhanga, the sun and the moon. These lesser gods share in Kiteme's power even though they are created beings. Thus the ancestors are able to appeal to the guardian power of Iryoba and Nyamhanga in order to ward off the evils that plague humankind. So the source of the power of the ancestors is their closeness to the guardians of the world, Iryoba and Nyamhanga, the sun and the moon.

At the same time certain groups, for example the Luo, do not separate the ancestors from the sun and the moon or even from God when they are in trouble. They call upon them all together for help in times of need, praying:

> All-present God, Sun, our father, God, look. We are your people. We want to offer to you this sacrifice of our ancestors. We want to eat with all our fathers and grandfathers. Breathe on us a good breeze for the children and their mother. Chase away the power of the evil spirit. May all the evil found in this homestead go into the sea.

However, upon reflection, no one would say that the great Kiteme could have any part in evil. To impute such a thing to Kiteme would be a blasphemy. God can only be good. For God to approve of or even to permit evil would be to make God less than God, would make God imperfect. God's creation is good and will remain good. Evil is the disorder arising out of the foolishness of God's creatures who can freely disturb that order. All that is needed to rectify evil is to restore the order that Kiteme created. The power to restore that primal order resides in the sun and the moon. If you argue that this power ultimately comes from Kiteme, you are right. However, to my mind, this does not prove your argument that God is involved in evil. God's power to conserve the order of the primal creation is exercised through Iryoba and Nyamhanga.

Furthermore, Padri, I hear you agreeing with me that it was the personal immorality of the first parents that caused the present disorders in the world. However, you then go on to say that some of the disorders are outside the control of the human will and, therefore, had to have come from another source. But what is that other source? Surely it cannot be from God who is the powerful one and completely good. Yet, that is what you imply in your teachings. Namely, that there is a hidden plan underlying evil, known by God, that makes reasonable unjustifiable sufferings and evil. Moreover, you say that, in the end, God will right all wrongs in a final judgment. Thus, if God knows this plan, then God somehow wills it or at least permits it. This leads one to say that the Christian God is actively involved in some of the evils that afflict humankind. To my way of thinking, therefore, the Christian God is partly evil because that God allows innocent creatures to experience traumatic suffering and pain while remaining silent. Where is your God as the rains fail in Ethiopia, the Sudan, and Tanzania? Is God's power for good, in fact, limited? Is God unable to stop and change what you call cosmic forces of evil that afflict humankind? Your Christian God seems to be a limited God with little or no power over evil.

MISSIONARY: Riana, in your question about the power of God over evil and God's involvement with it, I must say that you have touched on a mystery that even I find hard to accept and comprehend. It is as though we have all the parts of a bicycle in front of us, but we don't know how to put them together. We believe, on the one hand, that God is absolutely good and cannot do evil. On the other hand, we also believe that all creation obeys God and is subject to God's power. However, if this is true, why does the divine power not put an end to evil here and now, get rid of malaria, stop the famine, and stop the wars? Why does the goodness of God not lead God to have pity and mercy on the sufferings of the children, the crippled, the hungry? Our Christian God seems to be silent, to be deaf and dumb in times of problems, crises, and evils. The only hope held out is that no matter how difficult and painful things might be, we believe that some day there will be a release, and that all evils will be punished.

Yes, Riana, I think you have raised an important point. Christianity does not really protect the goodness of God when we are discussing evil, nor does it offer the living any immediate comfort and relief from the pains and sufferings of the present times. However, it does protect human freedom and personal responsibility for one's actions. Also, through the power of faith and love it offers a way of overcoming all evils, even death, through personal resurrection unto new life with God. This love is learned, practiced, and shared through discipleship with Jesus. Jesus is quoted as saying: "Take up your cross and follow after me and I will make your burden light." He also promised: "He who believes in me will have everlasting life."

Upon hearing my answer about overcoming evil through the power of faith and love, several of the Christians in the room voiced approval. One of them said that it took a very strong faith to resist turning back to traditional practices and rituals in times of serious troubles. Another said that it was only her trust in the power of Jesus that enabled her to accept the deaths of her four children in infancy. I nodded my agreement as I continued.

MISSIONARY: Riana, I want to question your idea that all evil is due to immorality. This teaching gives an unnatural and unnecessary explanation to many common evils that can best be understood as the result of poor judgments on the part of the people involved and it does not entail any moral elements. For example, a child wanders out into the road and is hit by a car and dies. What was the cause? Basically, the child was not properly supervised by an adult and happened to be in the wrong place at the wrong time. The only moral fault involved is the lack of diligence on the part of the one responsible. To look for some further reason, such as a person or spirit that caused the child to be in the road so as to be run over, does not make sense. There were no other wills involved except the child's and the guardian's. To look for another will as the source of evil seems to be unmerited by the circumstances and only serves to stir up accusations and hatred in the community.

I remember several years ago when a young boy of my village was found missing at nightfall. A cry of alarm went up, and every homestead sent out an armed adult to look for the boy. By morning the two clans in the village were at each other's throats, one claiming that the boy had been stolen by the other and killed in order to be used for witchcraft. Spears and clubs were held at hand, ready for fighting. At that point a schoolgirl returned with the boy. She had found him in a field halfway between his home and the neighboring village three miles away. The boy's mother had taken the same path the previous day to go off to work in her fields. Unknown to anyone, the youngster had tried to follow her and had been lost in the high grass.

Could this incident have been caused by another human being? Was this event sufficient to bring two clans close to riot and violence? No, Riana, many of the things that you say happen because of immorality are just chance occurrences due to the poor choices and judgments of individuals. Other people are not involved and cannot be involved. Your viewpoint leads to unjust accusations against innocent people.

RIANA: Mzee Padri, this question about the possibility of evil things happening due to the poor judgments and choices of human beings fails to see that from our perspective nothing happens by chance. Of course, we observe cause-and-effect relationships. For example, a bus goes off the road because the driver is going too fast, or a child dies because of a poisonous snakebite. But we do not accept that these actions happened by chance, or, as you say, accidentally. There are no chance happenings in this world. We must find out why the driver was driving too fast, and why the child was bitten. In the example you cited, we would question why the young boy went off looking for his mother. Through the answers to these kinds of questions, one encounters, as you say, the dark side of human nature, the faces of evil. Even in your example of the young soldier, the priest comforted his mother by telling her that his death in war did in fact have a meaning; it was not by chance. There was a reason why he died at such a young age. And this is exactly how we understand all evil. Nothing happens without a personal cause. To say otherwise, to my mind, would amount to denying the order and rationality of creation. Humanity is not trapped by fate or subject to irrational forces that inflict their evil without recourse. Such a vision of creation would make the creator, Kiteme, appear to be imperfect. It would show God's creation to be out of control, as if God had unleashed forces of evil that God no longer wishes to control or is unable to control.

Evil of all types, even that caused by bad judgments, is always the result of personal causes. Indeed, in the Luo language, there is no way of saying: "I have become sick"; rather, one says: "Someone has made me sick," and thus we search for the one who has caused the sickness.

Even you, Padri, in your teachings about Adam and Eve, give a personal cause for their banishment from the primal world. You say that it was their sin against the creator God that led them out of that world into this present imperfect world. But who created this so-called imperfect world? Surely Kiteme did not change his mind and convert his perfect creation into something imperfect. Nor did he create two worlds—one perfect and the other imperfect. The world as it came forth from the creator is one, good, beautiful, and sacred. It is this world. Thus the evils that befall humankind, even what you call cosmic evil, cannot be traced back to some kind of an imperfection in the work and power of the creator. To say otherwise is to undermine the power, wisdom, and goodness of God.

As I was listening to Riana's question, I realized how my own understanding of evil was limited and fragmented. I felt instinctively that the African explanation was just as logical and consistent as my own. I even wondered whether my problem with Christian teaching was due to my limited understanding of Christian theology or was built into the Christian understanding of evil itself. It seemed as if Christianity preaches a kind of fatalism in which evil is finally redressed only in another world—a true and final world. Also, Christianity seems to preach that, in this present world, God's power allows both good and evil. Because of this confusion, I found it difficult to answer Riana's question convincingly.

MISSIONARY: Riana, your question about the existence of two worlds, the primal world of harmony and the present world of suffering and evil, is very hard to answer. First of all, the two-world idea comes in the guise of a story explaining the rupture between God and humanity. It is like your stories of the creation where Kiteme once lived close to humanity and then withdrew due to some accident. The sufferings of humanity in this world are so overwhelming that they make a lie of the idea that God is absolutely good. So, to protect the goodness of God, the Adam-and-Eve myth developed in which humanity and not God is seen as the cause of the present state of the world. Indeed, God created a perfect place for humanity, but humanity rejected it out of pride and vanity. In this myth God remains a loving creator offering creatures a second chance at a better life and a way of overcoming evil. This myth also points out the radical freedom given to humankind—even the creator can be rejected.

So you see, Riana, this teaching seeks to protect the goodness and power of God while at the same time accepting that there is something radically wrong with the present universe. The present universe is full of moral and cosmic evils: sickness, disease, sin, and death, and it should not be that way. The Good News of the Christian religion is that these evils are only temporary. Furthermore, we firmly believe that a virtuous person, after death, goes to a world filled with divine harmony and order. Does this mean that one returns to the primal creation where God and humankind walked together in love and harmony? This we do not know. For hundreds of years our teachers have speculated on what the "new" world promised by God will entail. It is written in the Bible, our sacred book: "Eye has not seen, nor ear heard the joys prepared by God for those who love him." However, all agree that in the new world there will be no evil, and we shall be together with God and our loved ones.

At the same time, Riana, from what you have said, it seems that you also understand cosmic evil in a way similar to that of the Christians, namely, that ultimately cosmic evil cannot be contained or eliminated. I hear you saying that you know the cause, treatment, and prevention of all evils. However, often your remedies do not work and evils constantly recur. Did not the Kotuo villagers along the Mori River also throw their dirt into the river, asking that their village be protected from cholera? Yet forty people died there. Why did their rituals and prayers fail? And malaria, why can't you once and for all neutralize it? Why does it constantly come back to make you sick? So you are fooling yourself into thinking that you can control evil and fooling the people into paying a high price in money or cattle in order to ward off or conquer evils that simply cannot be warded off or conquered. They can only be temporarily neutralized. Many evils like drought come and go on their own and cannot be manipulated by even the most powerful medicines or rituals. In the end, evil is a mystery and cannot be entirely controlled by the living. This seems to be the only logical way to deal with it.

RIANA: Padri, your concern that our remedies for evil do not work and are merely a way to exploit the people touches an area of human existence that is hard to prove one way or another. If you consider that the people of Kotuo lost forty villagers to cholera, their prayers and rituals seem to have failed to stop the disease. However, if you consider the hundreds that lived and did not die, the remedy worked. The whole village could have been infected and all could have died. So the remedy did protect a substantial part of the village. And again, there was a reason why the forty died. There was some immorality involved that was not addressed that led to the death of these individuals. The remedy for cholera was indeed effective and was seen as such by the community.

At times it might seem that a remedy is too late, as in the case of a sudden death of a loved one. Yet, even in such cases, if the immorality had not been identified, then the evil would have continued wreaking its havoc on the living through death, infertility, chronic sickness, and major diseases.

Furthermore, to say that evil is everybody's problem—both those who are virtuous and those who are evil—implies that prosperity is not a judge of one's morality. Yet our experience has been that the evil person cannot prosper because one's evil actions carry an inescapable immediate sanction—there is no delay in retribution. Indeed, the evil person is always at war with those he or she is injuring as they counterattack with powerful charms and medicines to neutralize the evil power. Thus prosperity must be a sign that a person is in harmony with one's neighbors and is at peace with creation. And even if one abuses power over one's neighbors, everyone knows that within a reasonable time the ancestors will intervene and right the evils done. I recall a former district commissioner who oppressed the people by stealing cattle, land, and resources. The people waited patiently, knowing that he would fall on hard times. And sure enough, just a short time after he had retired, the bus on which he was traveling was sideswiped by a truck and he was split in two by the impact. Nobody was surprised.

With this story many of the people began to name the person involved, and they voiced approval of the interpretation of his fate. He was indeed rebuked by the ancestors for his evil ways. Some mentioned the injustices that they had experienced at his hands, such as when he forced each family to contribute a cow for a school that was never built—injustices that have now been punished.

Riana continued the discussion with a question.

RIANA: Padri, in your final solution to the problem of evil, I hear you saying that there are two camps—the camp of the saved with

God and the camp of the damned with the devil. But why do you need a creature like the devil to explain evil? Furthermore, what evidence is there to prove the devil's existence? Is the devil the evil part of the Christian idea of God? That is, do you in fact teach that there are two gods: the god of evil and the god of good? At least that is the way your teachings come across. Indeed, you even talk of a place of fire where the sinners will live forever in anguish with the devil. So even the totally evil devil will exist forever. Does not this give the devil divine qualities? Why does your God not destroy the devil once and for all the way a man will kill and destroy a leopard decimating his sheep or cattle? Are you teaching that there are two gods in competition for control over the lives of the living? Furthermore, why should your Christian God be so unsure of the goodness and loyalty of humankind as to lead it into temptation?

MISSIONARY: Riana, I think you are right in saying that Christianity seems to give the devil much power and influence, that at times the devil is like another god—the god of evil. Again I can only repeat our belief. The devil is not God but is a creature of God. The devil is totally dedicated to evil and will continue to exist even into eternity. The reason why God has allowed the devil to function in the land of the living is a mystery. Why God does not stop the devil's power once and for all, we do not know. Some of our teachers suggest that this world is a testing place for the virtue of each person—to see if one is worthy of eternal life. Without some hardship and difficulty, it would be difficult to separate out the good from the bad.

Other teachers see the devil as a nobody, a nothingness, the source of self-illusion and rationalization, the source of systematic evil for which nobody is responsible. Others feel that the devil itself is merely a myth created to personalize all the evil feelings and desires that are in human hearts and minds. They say that the devil is not a personal force, it is merely a fiction of the imagination, created to excuse both God and humanity from ultimate responsibility for evil by locating the source of evil in a cosmic nonhuman entity.

At the same time I am wondering if your African witch is any more real than the Christian devil. It seems to me that the witch is also a personification of all the evil feelings and hatred found in the human community. I am even wondering, Riana, if the witch truly exists.

Recently my students asked people in various villages if they knew of any witches. All replied affirmatively. However, when asked who they were, the people usually pointed out some old, morose man or woman who seemed to be living apart from the community. When asked to prove their case, none admitted to having had any direct experience proving that the person was a witch. They just took it for granted that these people were witches because of their unsocial behavior. None had any proof. Likewise, no one admitted to having ever seen a true witch, called a night witch, although all were certain that they existed. It seems to me that witches are figments of your imagination, created to put a human face on evil so that you can control it. But Riana, evil is not controllable, and to call old, sick people witches is to abuse the elderly. Often the so-called unsocial behavior of the old is due to chronic illness, senility, and exhaustion.

A woman I know is reported to possess an "evil eye." If she looks on a child in a certain way, the child will be harmed. Her eyes have a reddish tint—a sign of witchcraft. She confided to me how difficult it is to live in peace in her community because of these accusations. She has no intention or desire to harm anyone. Her eyes are red due to a chronic eye disease. She feels she is being unjustly accused by the community and is without any recourse. She does not consider herself to be a witch.

Where are the witches? Is there anyone who would admit to being a witch? Is there anyone you know who is definitely a witch? No, Riana, witches do not exist, as far as I can see. Your idea of witchcraft as a source of evil does not have any basis in reality. It is a false explanation.

With this attack on the existence of witchcraft, people in the house began to get a little nervous. It was only years later that I came to understand that even to talk about witchcraft meant that one was involved in it. Furthermore, the penalty to publicly name a witch is death.

Suddenly, to the anxiety of many, it was reported that an owl, a powerful symbol of witchcraft, had just landed in a tree behind the house. Many immediately got up and left. Even Riana seemed a bit upset and looked to the approval of the few elders who remained before answering.

RIANA: Mzee Padri, to deny the presence of witches in the human community is a serious matter and cannot go unchallenged. I think you have some primitive idea of what a witch looks like, and how he or she acts. That is, you expect to be able to identify a witch on sight. However, such is not the case. A witch harms others through his or her evil feelings of jealousy, envy, hatred, and anger. Indeed such feelings, once set loose, seek out and wreak havoc on the victims. Of course, no one would admit to being a witch until the evidence is overwhelming any more than one would admit to being a thief until caught with the evidence. Indeed, the power of these people for evil is so strong that they are able to disguise their true nature and appear as normal people so as to have the freedom to do their evil deeds. And how do we know that they exist? We see the evil that they cause; our diviners point them out; they are occasionally caught and confess their evil ways; they are sometimes killed by the community for self-protection. Mzee, witches are as real as evil itself. Witness the owl landing in the nearby tree, the familiar spirit of night witches. Is that not proof enough of their existence? And to say that the elderly are abused and called witches unjustly fails to understand that most of the elderly are highly respected, and that the people singled out have given cause by words or actions that indicate their involvement in witchcraft. Accusations of witchcraft are never made randomly, nor are they made by strangers. The problem concerning the existence of witches is yours not mine.

The conversation about evil ended on this note. It was getting late, and all were tired. Riana and I thanked one another for the interesting session. We both agreed that the problem of evil needed further discussion, because we were just getting into some of the major issues on the topic.

We shook hands vigorously as we parted. Riana again promised to come and visit the mission station as soon as he was feeling better. Some of the Christians invited me to spend the night. A few children begged for a ride on the motorcycle, and, when I began to drive slowly out of the compound, they ran alongside for a short distance shrieking happily. As I rounded the last turn leading out of the village, a valley unfolded on my right and, in the far distant corner, the tin roof of the mission church reflected the fading light of the evening sun.

COMMENTARY

In this conversation, Riana is not looking for a transcendental solution to the problem of evil because God cannot in any way be involved in evil. For him, all evil is within the human community and represents a disruption of the order of creation. All evil is linked to human immorality. The answer to evil is found within this present world. I, on the other hand, distinguished evil into two kinds, the evil caused by immorality and that caused by nature or the cosmos. This model of evil fits in with the two-world cosmic vision of Christianity and it allows the theologian to project onto the "other" world answers and questions about evil that cannot be resolved in terms of the present world—questions such as the final judgment of sinners and justice for the innocent.

The interesting thing here is that Western theologians are seeing fewer and fewer instances of cosmic evil. Even expressions of cosmic evils like major diseases such as malaria and bilharzia could be eliminated if the world community would put its resources into addressing this problem rather than into weapons. This shift in moral consciousness brings the Western theologian more in line with the African viewpoint that evil is one-dimensional, namely, moral, and that evil is resolved within the context of the present world. Even the tragic famine problem in Africa is being considered a moral evil rather than a cosmic evil because the world community demonstrates, through its ability to field, equip, and feed armies of millions of men, that it has both the technology and the resources to feed starving people in times of drought. Furthermore, there are ways of ensuring sufficient food for all if the world's resources were properly applied. This would eliminate the evil of famine from the world.

As Christian theologians begin to understand cosmic evils as part of the process of creation (some of which are now being conquered and neutralized by science, for example, smallpox), the paramount moral issue becomes impersonal, structural evils. These evils are hidden within social structures and institutions; they are evils for which nobody claims responsibility, yet in which many participate. In 1986 these kinds of evils were clearly seen in cases of fraud, involving major United States companies, in which the companies rather than individuals within the companies were declared to be immoral and were punished with fines—a travesty of justice. Riana, of course, would not accept evil as impersonal; people are responsible for their actions. Riana would have searched out and judged the guilty individuals in those companies—something that was done, in fact, after the public outcry over the injustices involved in the original settlements of the cases.

For Riana, the evils caused by the cosmos are paramount. The rural Africans live most of their lives on a subsistence basis where sickness and disease are the rule rather than the exception. A recent sampling of students at one rural primary school showed that close to 50 percent of the students had severe cases of malaria. The irony is that as a society develops and becomes more affluent, the moral evils increase as the cosmic evils decrease. In Western societies it is the moral evils that are out of control (witness the brutality and violence of the last two wars in "Christian" Europe), whereas in the African societies it is the cosmic evils that are most troublesome.

Theologically, as a young missionary, I was unprepared to come to grips with the cosmic evils that debilitate the African peoples. These evils were not important to me religiously, and I tended to deal with them medically and scientifically. This is a good example of how my local Western theology was out of step with major religious problems facing African peoples.

The issue of the symbolization of evil as witch or devil divided us. For Riana, in a very real sense, everyone potentially is a witch. The witch is "you-who-are-immoral." This refined moral sensitivity of the Africans should be a revelation to Western theologians who have tended to see traditional religious morality as impersonal and taboo-oriented. The fact that the witch is potentially any person shows how African morality is grounded in relationships within the human community and how it stresses, immeasurably, the moral responsibility of each and every individual. There is no "The devil made me do it" excuse in the African world.

The devil of the Christian religion is part and parcel of the two-world cosmic vision of Christianity. The devil functions as the evil link between the two worlds, reinforcing the belief that the ultimate solution to evil takes place outside this limited human existence. In this discussion, even though I mentioned the debate within Christian theology as to the nature of the devil, I took it for granted that the devil is a person with intellect and will who is actively involved in subverting creation. However, I now question whether this is an adequate and honest way to present Christian teachings on the devil. What is the Christian belief about the devil that should and must be proclaimed in the African church? Is not the witch, in the African context, the true symbol of the evil one, the father of lies, the hater of God, the devil of Christian revelation?

I also left unresolved the question of personal freedom and the power of God over evil even though this is a crucial dimension of Christian teachings about evil. I end up calling evil a mystery: God has power over it but allows it because of the nature of human freedom. As I told Riana, it is as though we have all the parts of the bicycle but do not know how to put them together.

Riana, with his "this-world" orientation toward life, does not really deal with the question of why people commit evil. He proclaims that God has absolutely nothing to do with evil but fails to see that the very possibility of evil has to be answered in terms of the kind of humanity created by Kiteme. If humanity is free to do evil, then God must be intimately involved in evil at least as the source of that freedom. This is an issue of African theology that needs a great deal of attention.

The translation of the word "devil" as "ancestor" by the early missionaries, in many of the indigenous languages, shows how out of touch they were with the traditional African worldview and religions. The confusion engendered is quite apparent in the scene where the woman was being exorcised. The people had clearly identified the word for "devil" with that of an ancestral spirit. Unfortunately, there is little evidence that the contemporary church in Africa is any more sensitive to these kinds of misunderstandings. There are just not enough missionary and African church leaders being trained as transcultural theologians and pastoral agents.

3

Widow Identity: Individual or Communal

Several weeks after our discussion on the problem of evil, Riana decided to accept my invitation and return my visit. He walked ten miles from his home to the mission station. The account of this journey was pieced together from various conversations.

As Riana left his home late in the morning he was accompanied by Lucia Akech. Lucia, the person I had originally stopped to visit, was the widow of his elder brother who had died over ten years before. Riana had taken her into his protection according to traditional customs. She had proved to be a happy addition to his homestead. The three children born of the relationship were legally the children of the deceased husband. Riana was proud that his brother's family continued to increase. It was some compensation for his untimely death by drowning while fishing in Lake Victoria.

Lucia gracefully carried a four-gallon tin of flour on her head as she walked along. A small baby was strapped to her back. Riana walked in front as was the custom. Little was spoken as they traveled. Six miles into the journey, the path from Riana's village joined a dirt road that ran through the middle of a village of four hundred grass-roofed homes. A few people greeted Riana as he passed by. All wanted to know where he was going. The supposition was that he had been called to help someone in need. He told them that he was going to the mission station to have a talk with the missionary. Someone shouted: "Oh, so you have become a 'reader!' " meaning one who is studying for baptism. "No," he answered, "but who knows what the future will bring. Maybe the missionary will become a 'reader' of the religion of our people." All smiled and wished him a good journey.

The road ended in a tee. Riana said good-bye to Lucia as she turned left, telling her to meet him at the mission station on her way back. Riana turned right and shortly entered the village of the Catholic mission station. People along the way were pleasantly surprised and happy to see him. His reputation as a diviner was well known. There were few in the area who had not benefited from his skills.

The mission station consisted of a church, painted red with white trim, and a large blue-and-white meeting hall, both one hundred by forty feet in size, lined up along the road. Tall eucalyptus trees dotted the property, providing shade and adding dampness to the tropical air. The missionary's house, which lay below the church, was almost hidden by a hedge that separated it from the church. It was the most substantial house in the village. It was made of cement blocks with a tin roof. It was painted light yellow with glass windows set in barred metal frames. In back of the house was a building containing a storeroom and a guest room, with a shed for two cars attached to the side. Next to the guest room was an outhouse. A large German shepherd dog was chained at the garage. It stirred slightly at the approach of Riana, who noticed that the dog's eyes were red—a sign of witchcraft.

I was in my room studying when Riana strolled into the yard, calling: "Hodi" (Hello). The mission cook, looking out the window, recognized Riana and greeted him with a clear "Karibu" (Welcome). The cook then called me, saying that Riana had arrived. I dropped everything immediately and went out to greet him. There was a look of happy surprise on my face. "Riana," I said, "Karibu sana" (A special welcome). We stood shaking hands, exchanging traditional greetings:

"Do you have life?"

"Yes, I have beautiful life."

"And your family, do they have life?"

"They also are with life."

In the end I said warmly: "Karibu ndugu" (Welcome, brother). Together we went into the building. The door led into a small office *containing a desk, a couple of chairs, a bench along one wall, and some large record-keeping books. The walls were painted and there were curtains on the windows. I invited Riana to sit down and then left to tell the cook to make some tea. When I returned we began our conversation.*

MISSIONARY: Riana, how nice to see you. I thought that maybe you would not take me up on my invitation because of what people might think if they saw you going to the Christian mission. Some might feel that you were interested in becoming a Christian and were no longer in touch with the ancestors. Others might think that your power to divine would be weakened if you associated too closely with Catholic priests who have all kinds of special Christian powers.

Riana smiled and answered that already people along the road were asking him if he were going to study for baptism. We both laughed at this matter. When it became apparent that Riana had come for a special visit and was not just stopping by on his way to some other place, I invited him into the living room of the house.

The living room had large louvered windows on one end, a sofa and two matching chairs, a couple of bookcases, a large dining table, and a buffet. There were pictures on the walls. We sat at the table as the cook brought tea and bread. Butter and jam were placed at hand.

As we drank our tea Riana mentioned that he had walked in with Lucia and that she had gone on to the local market where she hoped to sell or barter cassava flour for soap. She would be returning to meet him later on. I asked Riana if he was the one who had "inherited" her after her husband's death. He replied that he was. With that I remarked how the African custom of caring for widows seemed so strange—especially if the widow was a young person. I then began to question him about this custom.

MISSIONARY: Riana, why would a widow like Lucia not be allowed to remarry on the death of her husband? Why should she be left to live without a marital partner? I recall a young widow whose husband had been killed in the war with Uganda. She had been married only a few months before he died. Now she is in the care of her husband's brother. It seems to be unjust to force a widow to live the rest of her life without a husband. Why do you allow such a custom?

RIANA: Padri, this is the first time that I have heard our widow customs called strange. For me these customs are the only proper and normal way to care for the wife and family of a deceased brother. However, this is certainly an important issue, especially since the Christian churches have made it very difficult for widows to continue to practice as Christians after the deaths of their husbands.

For example, Lucia, my brother's wife, had been a Catholic leader—the chairperson of a small Christian community—before the death of her husband. Then, after his death, when she officially came under my care, she was not allowed to eat the bread served in the church. Lucia was very upset at the time and tried to work out a living arrangement that was acceptable to the priest and the Christian community. They told her that if a house were built for her outside the hedge of my compound, it would be a sign that she was not living with me like a wife but was merely under my protection. Lucia thought it over and then refused to attempt it. She realized that if she lived outside my compound she would be seen as an unfaithful wife who refused to follow the customs protecting her and her family. In addition the community would look down on her and she would be bothered by men looking for a casual sexual partner. In the end she told me that it was better for her to live with me in honor and decency than to live like a prostitute. I heard later that she told the priest that she still believed in Jesus and the church and, even though she couldn't receive the church's bread, she would remain a faithful Christian. Then, when she was past child-bearing, she would return to eat the bread once again.

Now, to me these Christian customs are strange. Why should the Christians be so hard on widows? Widows have enough problems on their own. You would think that the church would go out of its way to accommodate them.

MISSIONARY: Riana, I see that this problem has affected even your family. Let us talk about it to see if there can be some understanding. I think your customs are strange and you think the Christian customs are strange. Who is right in this matter? Let us go out on the veranda and talk about our different ways of caring for widows. Maybe we can find a common basis for understanding and appreciating each other's viewpoint.

Together we walked outside onto a brick-covered patio. The patio had a round charcoal grill in the corner and, in the middle, a table with four metal chairs and a beach-style umbrella. Several women standing by the church shouted greetings upon seeing us. They quickly walked down to the patio to greet us by hand—a clever way of inviting themselves to the discussion. Already the word was out that the famous Riana was visiting the mission. A few children began to appear out of nowhere. Riana began the conversation.

RIANA: Mzee Padri, let me start by telling you what marriage itself means to Africans, because the customs regarding widows make sense only in that context. You see, when people marry, there is the unspoken agreement with the family of the husband that this relationship will survive even his untimely death. That is, the man's family pledges to carry on the marriage by caring for the wife and children in the event of the husband's death. This is a very sacred and essential part of our marriages. This is why the families of both the bride and the groom are very concerned that the partners are properly selected and carefully scrutinized prior to any agreement for marriage.

Indeed, it is through marriage that one becomes an adult, that one takes responsibility before the community for passing on the gift of life, the greatest gift that one has received from the great Kiteme. Life is not a personal possession that one can manipulate for one's own purposes. No, life is a shared reality received from the ancestors to be passed on to the next generation. For one not to take this obligation of passing on life seriously implies that one is not an adult, that one is still a child, untried and without identity. In our language you cannot properly greet an unmarried adult. There are no words to identify an older person who is not married. I often have to smile when I hear people calling older Catholic sisters *nyako* (an unmarried girl), but what else can you call them? Indeed, for one not to found a family is seen as selfish and unsocial behavior.

Yes, Padri, it is through our marriage rites that the adult world is entered, controlled, shaped, and lived. It is the central institution that sets the tone for our whole society. Without marriage, we would be a people without roots, without stability, and without responsibility. We would be little better than animals that breed promiscuously. And this is why marriage is the concern of more than just the bride and the groom—it is the concern of the lineal families of both partners. Marriage is the means through which the lineage continues to grow and prosper. A lineage without marriages or without children is doomed, tragic, and cursed. A lineage with marriages and with children is blessed, happy and full of all good things. There is nothing in this world that can substitute for marriage and children.

Our whole lives are oriented toward marriage, family, and children. For example, if you want to know the sex of a new-born baby you ask in the Luo language: *"Okelo dhok?"* (Did someone bring cows?) If the reply is affirmative, it means that it is a daughter— one who will bring cows to the village when married. If it is a son, the response is *"En siro"* (i.e., the pole that holds up the roof of the house)—because sons stay with the family and support the parents in their old age. Likewise, when a woman gives birth to her first son, it is said: *"Onyuolo woungi"* (She has given birth to her father), meaning that this first son will care for her in her old age as her father cared for her as a girl. And, my brother, there are many more sayings such as these that would illustrate my point.

Customarily the families decide when it is time for a boy to marry. A member of the family is designated to find a suitable girl. The health of the girl's family in terms of mental illnesses, leprosy, or antisocial behavior is carefully scrutinized to determine whether or not the girl would be a proper choice. At times a father pledges a young son or daughter to a future marriage out of friendship or even to satisfy a debt. The friendship marriage is called, in Luo, *osiep kong'o* (friendship of beer) as the pledge often takes place around the beer pot. When the child becomes of age, then the marriage ceremonies begin.

Once a suitable partner is selected, the families arrange a meeting to work out the details. The boy and girl also meet to see if they are willing to go ahead with the arrangements of their parents. If there were some strong negative feelings on the part of either, these feelings would be taken into account. There is no need for the couple to spend time together prior to the beginning of the wedding ceremonies, for it is felt that true affection arises only through living together. To expect that the couple could make their own choices unaided is a misunderstanding of the nature of marital relationships. Indeed, formerly there would occasionally be a young boy who would insist on a girl against his or her parents' wishes. He could shame his parents into accepting his choice through kissing the girl's breasts in public. But this was rare indeed. Nowadays, due to the prolonged contacts of the children in the schools, more and more of the children wish to pick their own partners independently. To force the hands of their parents, some young people elope and run off to live in the towns and then, afterward, come back to settle up with their families. This new custom has hurt the stability of our family units.

Once the families accept a marriage arrangement, they begin the process of agreement through which expensive gifts are given to the bride's father. These gifts of cattle, goats, sheep, money, clothing, blankets, and even pots and pans represent the life inheritance of a particular person and show how the customs that cement the marriage bond are important and sacred. Indeed, to live with a girl without paying bridewealth is not tolerated in the rural areas even to this day. A young man in such a relationship is seen as a thief. The girl can leave him whenever she wishes and she takes the children with her. Children of such a union would be seen as bastards, without identity, without roots, without family, and of no advantage to the group. However, the giving of bridewealth is not the buying of the bride as you might suspect. No, it causes the girl to stay in her husband's village; it makes the marriage known to the girl's parents. Bridewealth is so necessary that if it is not paid, the marriage is not considered real or respected and the woman is not a wife. At the same time, bridewealth is compensation to the girl's family for expenses incurred in raising her. Likewise, one of the bride's brothers uses the bridewealth to marry his own wife. This creates a special relationship of trust and respect between them. The bridewealth also ensures that any children born of the union belong forever to the lineage of the father. So, my brother, marriage does not come cheaply in our traditions. It involves our whole economic system as well as our system of relationships. Bride-wealth is a gift, a pledge of friendship, a sign of a real marriage as well as a payment and a price. Is it any wonder, then, that our marriages are usually stable? Who would want to take these steps, to pay these gifts, more than once in a lifetime? The new bride, therefore, comes into her husband's family with the goodwill, expectation, and joy of the whole community. Everyone works to help integrate her into the life of her new family. A married couple is selected as the guardian couple to help the new marriage in times of stress. The wife, of course, maintains her relationships with her father's family, but she takes on the identity of her husband's lineage through her children. She is called an *ogwang'* (a mongoose), since she is like a mongoose in having two homes.

Once the marriage negotiations have been completed, the bride-groom and his friends begin to move some of the cattle to the homestead of the girl's father. In fact, the words "to marry" in the Luo language mean literally "to take cattle to a girl's homestead." When the cattle reach a certain number, about eight or ten, the bridegroom arranges to go at night and capture the bride away from her father's village. The girl will put up a commotion showing how much she loves her family—not to do so would be disgraceful. Then she runs off with her new husband to his village. In the Luo tradition, Mzee Padri, it is so important that the new bride be a virgin that an older couple witnesses the first act of intercourse. If she is found to be a virgin, the word is passed to the young bridesmaids waiting outside, who begin to shout and sing the praises of the girl and her family. The following morning the young girls run to the village of the bride's parents, singing songs of praise: "Look at them, everybody—parents who know how to raise their children. Their daughter has become a bride without ever sleeping with a man. Look at them, everybody!"

By this time a crowd of fifteen men and women had gathered near the patio. The customs about virginity caused many to smile, more out of embarrassment than shame. Matters such as these are usually not mentioned in a public gathering.

I have talked to some African elders who feel that the virginity of new brides in the Luo tradition seems to have given the Luo women a dignity and respect that is not given to women from other ethnic groups. In fact, some feel that the strength of the Luo culture and its ability to hold together in times of stress and war is directly related to the sexual discipline and fidelity of the women.

Everyone listened attentively as Riana continued with his explanation of African marriage traditions.

RIANA: This is the way, Padri, that the marriage starts. The bride and groom remain in the homestead of the boy's parents, learning to live together in love and harmony. The parents and other adults stand as role models to the new couple for the proper kind of adult behavior. Often the new bride is homesick for her father's place. The key person in helping the girl adjust to her new surroundings is the mother-in-law. However, if the mother-in-law finds the girl to be incorrigible, there is a good chance that the union will not last, especially if the couple continues to live in the rural homestead.

In our tradition, therefore, it is through living together that affection and understanding arise. It is the "hearing of one another" that is critical, not the possession of one another's time and attention. Love for us is the total acceptance of a person in one's various moods, and with one's needs and feelings. And how, you might ask, do we express this love? It is expressed through mutual understanding and love, care in sickness, the obedience of the wife, the giving of food and clothing to the wife, laughing together, talking together, the man's respect for his wife, and their cooperation in raising the children. Indeed, if you ask an adult who is the person's best and most intimate companion, the overwhelming majority will tell you it is one's husband or wife (wives). And if you ask them what causes troubles in marriages, they will tell you it is primarily due to incompatibility, then infidelity, beatings, drunkenness, and, lastly, problems over food and money.

Is the African woman a pawn in the power of her husband? In no way. She is seen as the life of the village, the cook, the one who gives birth and makes the household grow, the one who does everything. Living with her husband makes her one with him. Indeed, both of them wanted the marriage. If the woman has no husband, she has no children. In marriage both are having children—the greatest good.

On the other hand, the husband also has his responsibilities and work. He builds the house, plows the fields, is the head of his wife and the leader of the village; this is how men and women were created. If a man has bridewealth in his possession but no wife, he is most likely considered to be a witch, a perverted human being.

It is in this context that the children are born—each one seen as a reincarnation of an ancestor. Indeed, it is often said that the birth of a child is the death of an ancestor. And this is why a child is named after an ancestor and is often greeted as that ancestor, especially by the elderly. These children bring a fulfillment to the marriage process, proving that the ancestors are happy with the marriage. The wife grows into maturity and fullness of womanhood under the tutelage of the women in her husband's village. She finds her adult identity as the wife of her husband and the mother of her children.

If the husband should have an untimely death, there is no desire on the part of the wife to leave her home and search for a new lineage in which she could become a wife. Why? Because in our society marriages are forever, even beyond the grave. The husband's death was not her doing. She is an innocent bystander. Furthermore, her children have their identity and their spirit names from their father. To take the children away from the father's lineage would be an injustice. They would grow up without roots, identity, and a place to belong. A widow could run off, leaving her children behind in her husband's homestead, but what kind of a woman is it that would want to abandon her own children?

Padri, it is in this kind of a marriage context that our customs for widows have meaning. The widow is taken in by one of her husband's brothers, who cares for her just the way her husband would have cared for her by providing food, clothing, shelter, children, love, and affection. In a real sense, the brother-in-law becomes a surrogate for the absent husband. Any children born of the union are legally the children of the deceased brother. For example, the three children born to Lucia after the death of her husband are called the children of my brother, not my children. It is in this way that the lineage ensures that the family founded by a brother is not truncated by death but continues to grow and develop. Eventually the widow ends up in the care of her eldest son—the same situation as a woman widowed in her old age. The customs for widows must be seen as temporary adjustments in the marriage of a deceased brother to ensure that his family achieves its goals as if he were alive.

Do not think, Padri, that the care of a widow is an easy thing. It is a sacred obligation and not easily undertaken. It makes more work and sacrifice for the brother and can take away energy from building up his own family. Indeed, if you ask people why a brother-in-law cannot marry a widow as a wife, some will tell you it is because she is already married and cannot be married twice; others will say that the bridewealth has already been paid—it isn't right to take cows to a girl's village twice. Others will answer that a widow cannot leave her children or that she did nothing that causes her to be removed from the family—death just took her husband.

I remember, a few years ago, that one of the catechists from the mission came to my village and asked a lot of questions about marriage. One of these questions was about the way the Christian churches forbid the custom of inheriting widows. Most in my village felt that this Christian prohibition was wrong. Some said that the church should allow a widow to practice as a full Christian because she still loves God, and God did not forbid this custom. Others said that a widow is not a prostitute but would become one if she was not under the care of her brother-in-law. Moreover, it is the widow's sacred duty to follow the laws of the ancestors, which protect her family and children. Likewise, she didn't kill her husband and there is no reason to reject her, for she is in need and should be helped to make her family grow and prosper. On the other hand, the church adds to her troubles and gives people bad ideas about her marital status. The church would have her husband's family throw away the bridewealth, give up the children, and drive the widow away to play the prostitute. In fact, they said, the widow remains in her husband's homestead because of her love for her husband and his family. Moreover, if one refuses to care for a brother's wife, it shows that you do not love your brother. Such a breach of trust could cause the deceased brother to put the evil eye on you and bewitch you, seeing how you have treated his wife and family unjustly.

As the diviner was finishing, a middle-aged woman, carrying a baby on her back and a four-gallon tin container on her head, appeared around the corner of the building. The dog was barking and she was looking back apprehensively. It was Lucia. I recog-

nized her and welcomed her. Handshakes were exchanged. Some-
one got up to give her a chair.

"*We were just talking about you, Lucia," I said beaming, "and*
about all the customs of your people in caring for widows. You
must have heard us on the road! How are things at the market?
What did you buy?"

Lucia showed a bar of cheap laundry soap that she had ex-
changed for flour. She seemed pleased that she was able to get the
soap as it had been in short supply for a long time.

As Lucia was getting comfortable and greeting various people, I
turned to Riana and asked if he still had more to add to his
description of customs regarding widows.

RIANA: Padri, there are many more things to add, but now it would
be best if you explain the Christian customs for the care of widows.
With Lucia present, she can help with the discussion. She knows
what it means to be a widow and be declared immoral by the church
because of her following traditional customs for the care and
maintenance of her family.

MISSIONARY: Riana, this question of the care of widows is certainly a difficult problem for the Christian churches. Many women
are in the same situation as Lucia. They can be faithful Christian
leaders one moment and the next rejected because of circumstances
outside their control. But what is the church to do? Should the
church accept the widow customs and ignore its own special teachings about the nature of marriage? Let me start from the beginning
and explain our beliefs about marriage; then, maybe, you can see
why we deal with widows the way we do.

As Christians we believe that when a person is born, God gives
that person a new, unique life. It is not the life of an ancestor. It is a
new creation. Thus a person has his or her own value from within.
It is not given them either by society or by the ancestors. Therefore
we feel that the rights of a unique person cannot be subordinated to
the rights of the community, whether it be the clan, the society, or
even the family. It is only when an individual begins to violate the
personal rights of another that society steps in to arbitrate, punish,
imprison, or fine. We feel that this view of humankind is part of
our Christian heritage, part of the freeing message brought by

Jesus Christ. Thus, no matter how humble and poor one might be by birth, or how weak and sick one might be through suffering and disease, all have equal beauty and rights before God.

As a child grows older, these personalistic values are taught formally in the schools and informally in the home. Children are taught that they should fully develop all their talents because these talents are God-given. Of course they are taught concern for society and public order, but this concern is often more out of utilitarian values than out of genuine concern for others. Public space is not sacred space. One respects the public order out of enlightened self-interest. The rules of the society are kept so that public space is available for one's own development and entertainment whenever and wherever that might be.

In the question of marriage, this same kind of personalistic outlook is central. We feel that marriage is a personal matter between two people. Marriages are not arranged. The two people discover each other as suitable marriage partners through a process called "courtship" in which they meet and share together over a period of time. Once they feel their relationship is such that they are ready to make a permanent commitment to one another as husband and wife, they notify their families and friends of their marriage intentions. Their families rarely try to stop the marriage. Their families, of course, are concerned that they are compatible and happy but, because each couple lives independently of their parents after marriage, the parents do not have any ongoing influence over the development of the relationship.

We say that one must first be deeply in love with a person before deciding to marry, and that marriages fail when this personal love stagnates or ceases. In many ways, however, this kind of personal love tends to become possessive. It often demands all the time and attention of the partners. It is never satisfied. It always seeks greater sharing and oneness with the partner and it cannot tolerate long separation. As a result, many of our young people find it difficult to develop such a love relationship and live in such a rarefied atmosphere simultaneously. In reality, intense personal romantic love is only temporary. The long-term marital living and loving together still has to be learned. But our family situation is such that there are no live-in models for adult marital behavior after marriage, and each couple is left to work out its particular problems on its own. Often the social norms and pressures of their peers are the most important influence on their relationship. This is not a very efficient way to develop a marital relationship, yet we see this kind of marriage tradition as liberating and freeing from the authority of the adults. We see it as a good way to marry and found a family. In fact, we tend to see it as the only reasonable way to do so.

However, there are many who feel that our family structures create a type of individualism that is destructive of personal values. They feel that the very elements of individual freedom and independence, upon which we pride ourselves, do not represent any breakthrough in human development. Rather, these elements promote a kind of personal immaturity that leaves people in a state of perpetual adolescence. To address these problems, the Christian churches support various kinds of activities such as the Catholic Family Movement, Marriage Encounter groups, and special days of prayer and reflection, which are aimed at helping people develop their marriage relationships according to Christian ideals: intimacy, faithfulness, love, and fidelity. The very existence of these groups shows that our Western culture is far from promoting Christian marital values.

In place of responsible adults within the extended family to help relatives in times of difficulties, there are numerous agencies funded and supported by the government. Thus if the head of a family is out of work, there is a government-regulated unemployment service to help out financially. If the husband should die, the widow can claim a certain amount of financial help and aid from the government for herself and her children. There are also counseling services available to help with problem children, with excessive drinking or abusive behavior on the part of a spouse, or with marital incompatibility. The relatives of a particular family may or may not help in these matters. It all depends on the quality of the personal relationships among the individuals. There is certainly no obligation on the part of the relatives to help.

Likewise the birth of children is seen mainly as a private affair—the couple expressing their love in a concrete personal way through their offspring. Indeed, most couples these days decide how many children they wish to raise and limit their families through some form of birth control. There is little thought of fulfilling their obligation to continue their family line, much less the human race. Most couples do not have a sense that they ought to procreate in order to pass on the gift of life. This outlook and attitude toward children leaves parents in our Western society with the complete responsibility for the socialization of their children. As a result there is only one father figure and one mother figure as role models for the developing children.

The children receive their inheritance of money and property from both parents but even this is subject to legal arrangements. That is, a parent can decide not to leave his or her property to the children and can leave it to others. This often happens when parents are estranged from their children. In some sense, leaving one's children with nothing is a type of revenge from beyond the grave. So you see, Riana, our individualism reaches even to the matter of the family's wealth. Its distribution depends on the will of the individual, and this, we feel, is the way it ought to be. Each individual is a self-contained, independent economic unit who is to use his or her talent to the fullest to attain the good life. If one should fail, then the government is available to help.

A family founded by a man who has since died continues through the efforts of his widow. She must now be both a mother and a father to the children. Often her family, or the family of her husband, will give her help, but it is all voluntary; it is not owed. If she wishes, she can begin looking for a suitable partner to enter into a new marriage. If this happens, she brings her children with her to the new marriage, as does the new husband. Sometimes the children will be legally adopted by the new husband and take his family name—especially if they are young. Otherwise they keep the family name of their deceased father. I know of one case where a widow brought six children to a new marriage and the husband five, making a new instant family of eleven children.

So, Riana, it is within this personalistic approach to marriage and adult life that our customs for the care of widows has meaning. When the husband dies, we believe that the widow becomes free to establish a new household and found a new family. She can even legally marry her brother-in-law. Marriage is always a personal choice. It cannot be forced by society or by clan rules and customs. In the meantime, the widow's children remain with her for identity and inheritance even in the event of a new marriage. At the death of her husband, the social and religious ties that bound them together are seen as ended. In fact, in the Christian marriage ceremony the couple explicitly pledges fidelity and loyalty only "till death do us part."

At the same time, death is seen as the only way to dissolve a marriage so that the living partner can marry again. Even if a couple has not lived together for years, the Catholic Church maintains that they are still married and cannot validly marry another. However, the death of a spouse frees them to remarry. One of our early teachers, St. Paul, writes clearly that he would prefer that widows do not remarry. However, he says, if they cannot live chastely without a marital partner, it would be better to marry than to live sinfully and ultimately to burn in hell, the place of Satan.

With this, I paused as I realized how strange my words must have sounded to Riana. What could "burning in hell" possibly mean to the old diviner? Moreover, the very idea of marriage ending at death was something foreign to Riana's way of thinking. I also realized that my analysis of marriage and widowhood was more rambling than systematic—I had never thought out these matters. The ways in which widows are cared for in my society were never questioned; they were taken as the ordinary normal pattern of behavior. I wondered how much of what I had said made sense to those listening.

At this point my cook interrupted the gathering by announcing that food was ready. I invited Riana, Lucia, and several of the older men and women into the house. The rest broke up into little groups and continued the discussion. None of them showed any desire to be invited. This was the proper way to serve food to a special guest. The people's conversation fixed on my idea that a woman could be married more than once. Most thought it very strange. As we sat down to eat, Lucia spoke up.

LUCIA: Padri, what you have just said about widows does not make sense to me. I remember that when my husband, Joseph, died a missionary told me to go and get remarried. At the time I thought that he just did not understand our customs. Now I hear you, ten years later, repeating the same thing. Has anybody studied this problem? Do you see any Christian widows getting remarried?

It is difficult enough to be left a widow without being rejected by the church. Is it not written in the Bible that "charity pure and undefiled before God is to help widows and orphans in their needs"? How is the church responding to that biblical mandate? In my case the church turned on me when my husband died and declared me to be an immoral person living in sin with Riana. What kind of charity is that? Is there any other decent way for a widow to live? Did you want me to abandon my children, force my father to return the bridewealth, and have my husband's family send me home in disgrace? Are not the children raised up in the name of my husband a proof of the goodness of our customs? Padri, my marriage has not failed. It continues on even though the church declares me to be a sinner. But what is so sinful? How can one change one's lineal family, one's identity? These realities last far beyond the grave!

MISSIONARY: But don't you see, Lucia, Christianity has its own unique rules and ways, and as religious leaders we usually just follow the teachings of our particular church. It is only recently that we have been made aware of the fact that most of our teachings have developed over the centuries and that many particular customs, such as our family customs, were shaped more by economic and social necessities than by Christian doctrine. Some of our teachers are just beginning to understand that humanity is composed of thousands of cultures, each with its own unique marriage rites and customs, and it is these rites and customs that must be accepted and integrated into Christian life if a universal sense of God's revelation and presence is to be realized. Indeed, the way the independent Christian churches in this area are adapting Christianity to traditional family values and rituals gives us an insight into how this kind of indigenization can take place. Maybe it would be possible for the church to follow traditional customs for the care of widows if the issue were properly debated and understood. However, at this point, there is no possibility for this kind of change. None of the African or missionary bishops would agree.

Riana, what do you think about all this?

RIANA: Mzee, the marriage customs of your people seem to contain a tragic flaw. To think that life is a gift given to an individual as his or her own personal possession fails to comprehend the nature of human procreation. The helpless baby at birth is totally dependent on the care and concern of the family. It cannot talk, walk, or help itself. It only knows how to feed by sucking. The life force of the baby grows and increases only with the care of the family. It is clear to all that the nurturing of this one new life is a nurturing of life itself—the great gift of Kiteme given to the family to be shared. Human growth and life are inconceivable without the family community. The family community is the greatest asset of humankind. There is no identity outside the community. Why, then, does Christianity take such a strange stand on marriage, the building block of the community? It seems to me that even though you attempt to minimize the role of the blood community in the development of a family, you turn around and substitute the government and the church with all its social services in place of that community. My friend, marriage cannot be an individual affair outside the control of the families of the partners. Marriage exists to build up the lineages through sharing the life of the ancestors with the new generation.

With Riana's reply, the conversation quickly ground to a halt as the pleasures of eating took priority. When the meal was finished and several of the elders had moved outside, Riana got up and exchanged a few words with Lucia as to when they should start back. They agreed that it should be shortly. All returned to the veranda, and the people outside again gathered around. I called on all to be quiet and began to respond to Riana's last question.

MISSIONARY: One of the things, Riana, that Christianity has prided itself on is that individuals have equal worth before God. Thus one does not need to be linked to an ancestor or a relative in order to be whole. Wholeness and identity come from doing God's will and living in peace and love with one's neighbors. Of course, an infant is totally dependent on its parents in order to survive. However, the final state of the infant is not determined by its blood links or its family connections. Its life will continue beyond the grave either in grace with God or in sin with the devil. This is why we say that a new life is a new creation; it is not an ancestral creation. And I suppose this may be the root of the individualism that we now proclaim. At the same time we see how important family relations are. Indeed, in my own society in America, parents are decrying that the family has become fragmented and that the children are more influenced by their peers than by adults. In response the state government has taken a greater role in the growth, care, and development of the family unit. The result is such that even I would not feel any special obligation to help members of my family in need. I would feel that the government is the first and ordinary place for them to turn in times of trouble.

Returning to your explanation of widow customs, Riana, the thing I find most difficult to understand is how you can live with your brother's wife and pretend that you are acting for your brother. Surely marital relations are so intimate that one cannot act for another in such circumstances. It seems to me that you are just pretending that she is your brother's wife so that you can keep control of her children and your brother's wealth. In fact, she is for all intents and purposes your wife, whether first or last. These widow customs are more due to economic priorities than social or religious values.

LUCIA: Padri, I am not Riana's wife, I am the wife of his brother. Riana takes care of me in the name of, and with the implied consent of Joseph, my husband. There is no way that I could ever become his wife. Even the idea of having two husbands is repugnant. Marriage is once, forever. One never loses a spouse, even through death. The only way out of a marriage is through a divorce proceeding, even if one of the partners is dead. Really, to call me the wife of Riana is not only inaccurate but meaningless. Why do you feel that marital love is so exclusive that it cannot be shared with several people? Why do you feel that I cannot love personally both Riana and his brother? Why don't you understand that Riana merely takes the place of my husband? I can even call him by my husband's name. Ask Riana!

RIANA: As Lucia says, Padri, the caring for a widow is directly related to obligations to one's brother—he who shares your life and blood. If my deceased brother perceived me as trying to supplant him as the husband of Lucia, he would be angered and would send me serious troubles. Again, if I failed to take proper care of her, he likewise would be angry with me. Through these customs, the life and reality of my brother is kept alive through memory, through his children, his things, and his wife. Isn't this a fitting way to remember the dead? It is as if his shadow continues to be present to us beyond the grave. And why can I not substitute for my brother in raising up children to his name? He would have done the same for me if I had died first. How can one in justice blot out the reality of one's brother and allow his family and children to be lost? It seems that caring for the widow by plowing for her, building her a house, giving her food and clothing are praised by your church as Christian charity. But to help her develop her family through procreation is seen to be evil. This just does not make sense. A woman wants and needs her children as much as she wants and needs shelter, food, and clothing. So why does your church want us to respond to only part of the widow's ongoing needs? It seems to me that the only real charity to a widow is to respond to all her needs, to treat her in the context of her life and reality as a faithful wife—and this means raising up new children in the name of her deceased husband.

Everybody standing around nodded approval of Riana's point about the widow's desire for children. One elder recalled a meeting at one of the mission stations where the care of widows was carefully discussed. At the end of the meeting, there was general agreement that they could find nothing in the customs of widow inheritance that was against gospel values. An African priest at the meeting had said openly that he did not understand why it had been prohibited.

As the comments died down, I continued the discussion with another question.

MISSIONARY: Riana, you say that remarriage is impossible for a widow. Yet in this Mara district there are many widows who remarry among the people called the Wakwaya. They argue just the opposite from you as to the best way to care for widows. Their customs are very similar to those preached by the Christian churches. The Wakwaya say that there is nothing to stop the widow from remarriage when the husband has died. So it seems that this custom of yours is peculiar to your ways and manners and cannot be used as the norm for other African people.

RIANA: Mzee, what you say about the Wakwaya is right. Their widows do remarry. However, they have very different marriage customs. The woman's children inherit from their maternal uncle and not from their fathers. Thus the children build up the lineage of the mother; they belong legally and socially to the family of their mothers. Also, there is only a token payment of bridewealth given as a gift to celebrate the marriage rather than to determine the legal place of the children. So, even though they seem to be like us in their marriage customs, they are, in fact, very different. In a real sense the Wakwaya girl never breaks her ties with her natal family. At the death of the husband, there are no expensive gifts to return if the widow remarries, nor is there any need for the widow to leave her children behind when going into a new marriage. You know, Mzee Padri, the African people are not one culture. We have many diverse and widely different ways of viewing reality and dealing with some of the basic questions that confront humankind. For example, the neighboring peoples, the Masai, are very different in their ways of acting and living. Even you would find it difficult to communicate with them. We do not understand them at all. I have no idea how they would care for widows. However, I am sure it would be in terms of their marriage traditions. So, in answer to your question, the heart of the widow customs is the preservation of the ritual, legal, and social identity of the widow and her children. In the case of the Wakwaya, the remarriage of the widow does not alter her social identity or her children's identity. Hence the Wakwaya are not opposed to her remarriage.

Padri, even though it is time to start home, I still have one more question about your marriage customs. Why is it that you do not want your children to live with you after their marriages? It seems to me that you are trying to cut off your children right at the very point in their lives when they most need parental guidance and help. What kind of a lifestyle is it that seeks to live alone and isolated? How can there be any joy in a family without children, without young and old adults living together? How can one conceive of life alone? And how can children know who they are if their mothers go from lineage to lineage through remarriage? Mzee Padri, the good life is with and among people, your own people. Your custom of living alone after marriage seems to me to be a sign of rejection, hostility, and selfishness regarding your children. Your children were given you by the great Kiteme to nurture until your dying days, not counting the cost. Your kind of family organization seems to me to be rather sad and primitive. It doesn't take into account that responsible parenting is a work that never ends—it remains with one until the grave. It sounds to me as though you want your widows to remarry mainly because you do not want to take responsibility for them and their children. You do not want to keep them as a part of your homestead. If Christianity only teaches your Western ways of founding and organizing a family, then I think the African people should resist and reject Christianity with all their efforts.

MISSIONARY: Riana, I cannot help smiling at your comments. Why do you always end our discussions on a difficult point? Of course we love our brothers' widowed wives and their children, but we have no legal or social responsibility to take care of them. And why do we live apart from our children? Well, that is just the way we do it. It does seem strange that we want our children to leave us while we are still healthy and they are still maturing. Then, when we get old and become dependent, we complain that our children are disrespectful and do not care about us. Some of our teachers say that our Western kinds of family relationships promote instability and antisocial behavior. Others say that we live this way because of the economic order, which demands high mobility. Others feel that our way of living is entirely cultural and has little or nothing to do with Christianity. Christianity just tries to make the best of our peculiar type of family organization. And maybe you are right. Perhaps we should be more responsible for our widows and their children. Perhaps we should try to maintain the widows' identity as married women. Maybe your customs can teach us a new way of living and loving as Christians when dealing with the families of our deceased brothers.

All smiled as I finished talking. It had been a long discussion, but all seemed to have enjoyed it. I asked Riana if he would like to see the church building, but he declined because the sun was rapidly setting. Lucia had already strapped the baby to her back and was lifting the tin container onto her head. Handshakes and good-byes were shared with all. Riana picked up his cane and walked briskly out of the yard. Lucia followed closely behind. The dog by the cars moved to the end of its chain as they passed by but remained silent. Lucia watched it out of the corner of her eye. I stood talking for a few moments to several of the elders. Then they too went off. I turned and went into the rectory, the screen door closing behind me.

COMMENTARY

In this discussion the issue of the nature of personal and social identity is key. For Riana the foundation of adult identity is the lineal community through which life forces are shared. For me identity is understood in much more individualistic terms. From my point of view adult identity is a personal possession somewhat independent of the community that nurtured it. This basic difference has many implications:

Western Viewpoint	*African Viewpoint*
Life is a personal possession	Life is a communal reality
Marriage is not essential to adult identity	Marriage is essential to adult identity
Marriages end at death	Marriages continue beyond the grave
Love is possession of the loved one	Love is acceptance of the loved one
Marriage gifts go to individuals	Marriage gifts go to family of the bride
No responsibility to continue a widow's marriage	Ongoing responsibility to continue a widow's marriage

Children are a private affair	Children are a community affair
Only the parents are responsible for socialization of children	The whole lineal family is responsible for socialization of children
Marital love is learned independently with no live-in adult models	Marital love is learned through living and parental guidance
Government is the wider-support community	Clan is the wider-support community
Nuclear family is self-contained	Lineal family is community-contained

I now realize that what I was perceiving in this conversation as "innate" values regarding the structures of family and marriage are not innate at all; they are cultural. The African system of marriage and family makes just as much sense as my own Western system.

The major theological issue in this discussion is the meaning of the surrogate relationship between the widow and the brother-in-law in terms of sexuality. In traditional Western Catholic teachings on marriage, one can accept the brother-in-law's care of the widow and her children in everything except the sexual/procreative activity—sexual relationships and legitimate marriage are seen as necessarily linked. For Riana, on the other hand, there is no possibility of marrying a widow, and the sexual relationship with the widow is not only a duty but a dramatic sign of the seriousness of the family obligation to continue the deceased brother's family. It also symbolizes the belief that the dead are still living and are influential in the affairs of the living—an idea barely considered by contemporary Western Christianity.

Moreover, the surrogate relationship with the widow is not polygyny, as it has often been characterized. It is a temporary adjustment in the marriage of the deceased brother to ensure that his marriage achieves its goals. This kind of relationship has not yet been discussed adequately by theologians, mainly because it is just now being understood in terms of its uniqueness. The custom of widow inheritance is a clear example of how Western moral theologians were able to condemn and dismiss the custom by mislabeling it as a type of polygyny.

The central pastoral question is: What should be the response of the Christian churches to the care of widows in Africa? Should it be a qualified acceptance of the surrogate relationship with the brother-in-law? Should it be acceptance of the inheritance customs without restrictions? Should it be continuing opposition?

Western individualism in terms of family structures does not seem very attractive to Riana. He feels it is an irresponsible way to raise children, care for a family, and share life. This viewpoint questions some of the basic family values that the Western Christians have taken for granted as representing human growth and development in the area of identity and relationships.

In this conversation, even though we are both talking about familiar matters, we are further apart than in the two previous discussions. Each system of marriage has its own inner logic. If you attack or disturb a critical part of that system, you threaten the very system itself. The Christian church's encouragement of the remarriage of widows signifies a frontal attack on the fabric of many of the African family systems. Riana realizes this and responds by saying that the people should reject Christian teachings on widows with all their might.

It appears from this discussion that the lineal family structures of the African people are more personalistic and ordered toward promoting social and human life and, thereby, closer to gospel values than the individualistic Western family structures. Westerners tend to see ethnic group, clan, and lineal or extended family as limiting and the end of personal development. Africans take just the opposite stand: ethnic group, clan, and lineal or extended family are the source and root of a truly human existence.

4

Religious Ministry: Divination or Priesthood

After my first three conversations with Riana, I had been inter-ested in speaking with other diviners to see if Riana's vision of African life and religion was typical. The opportunity presented itself several weeks later in a village where I was staying as a guest of the Christians. The people pointed out five different diviners in the village. All of them were practicing their skills. The chairperson of the church arranged a late evening meeting with a diviner who had been baptized as a Catholic. His name was John. I was intrigued as to how a Catholic could become a diviner. I hoped that since he was a Catholic it would be easier to talk to him, as we would have a common religious faith. Also, I had hoped that the visit would be somewhat secret. I was afraid that if a lot of people gathered around, the spontaneity of the discussion would suffer.

After supper the chairperson and I made our way down a path to John's home. The sounds of night, the smell of cattle in the corrals, and the heavy, peaceful feeling of sleep filled the air. Occasionally strands of conversations were heard as we walked by particular households.

The mud-and-wattle home of the diviner was poor and shabby, and in need of major repair. The diviner did not look very well. He was dressed in a torn shirt. He greeted us warmly and invited us into his home. Small stools were offered as seats. The diviner's wife, dressed in an old white smock, also greeted us and then

*continued on with her work preparing food. There were chickens in
the rafters overhead that occasionally moved and cackled softly.
The sounds of the chickens led me to cast nervous glances at the
roost, afraid of droppings. My reaction was a source of amusement
to the diviner's wife who was grinding flour on a large stone. Light
was provided by the flickering flame of a kerosene lamp made out
of an old tin can.*

*In the beginning, the conversation was slow and labored. The
diviner was not sure why I had come. He thought that maybe there
was some problem with him or his family and he was being careful
to say the right things. He did not want to be on the wrong side of
the Christians.*

*After a time the conversation picked up, especially when some of
my questions about divination made the wife laugh. She could not
believe that someone could be so naïve and uninformed about
essential matters such as the source of a diviner's power. She would
nod to her husband with a look of absolute disbelief at my questions. Her reactions annoyed me and I didn't appreciate her humor.
Also, a few of the neighbors had arrived and were crowding in at
the door. They too shared in her humor. This further annoyed me.*

*Finally, after a bit of probing, I got John to tell the story of how
he had become a diviner.*

DIVINER: Mzee, when I was a young man, shortly after I had
become a Christian, I became seriously ill. The people prayed over
me, asking for my renewed health, but to no avail. Finally, in
desperation, I went to my uncle, a practicing diviner, to find out
why I was so sick. At that time I was close to dying. He immediately
found the cause. I was sick because I was being possessed by the
spirit of Ramogi, the founder of the Luo people. It was Ramogi
who was sapping my life strength. My uncle told me quite clearly
that unless I took the proper measures to ward off his power, I
would be killed. After a period of time I realized that the only way
to come to grips with this ancestral spirit was to agree to become its
medium, to speak its message to the people, to make present its
will. In return the spirit guaranteed that my health would return.
However, becoming the medium of an ancestral spirit was no easy
matter. I stayed for five years in the village of my uncle, apprenticing the ways of divination and learning how to keep a delicate

balance between the demands of the possessing spirit and my own sanity. I even learned through my uncle a special secret language that enabled me to converse with the spirit. At times the battle was overwhelming, and I almost died. Finally, I was able to work out a relationship with the intruding spirit that has guaranteed my survival. Now, when I divine for someone, it is the spirit possessing me, Ramogi, that tells me what to say and tells me which medicines to make or what sacrifices to offer to overcome the afflicting evil.

Being possessed by an ancestral spirit puts me in a special position between the living and the dead. I interpret and make present Ramogi's desires and needs. It is a difficult and dangerous work. At times Ramogi puts me into a trance and takes total control of my own spirit and body. I then speak Ramogi's words and do his deeds as he directs those who have come to me for help on how to overcome evil in their lives. Afterward the people pay me with gifts of food, money, or livestock in appreciation of the good results obtained. This ministry is essential to the health of the community. Without the good graces of the spirit world, there is nothing human that can be achieved and sustained. Things such as fertility, good crops, rain, health, and prosperity are all under the protection of the ancestors. Without their encouragement and consent, these things would not happen.

For example, many women come for divination in order to find the cause of their infertility. Often it is due to the breaking of a clan taboo, such as the improper burial of a person. I remember a case several years ago when only a few of the women of a particular clan were bearing children. Upon consultation with the spirits of the ancestors, it was revealed that the clan had buried a young woman several years previously at the mission station in an improper manner. The foreign doctors at a hospital run by Mennonite missionaries from the United States had said that the girl's death was due to a stomach tumor. However, to the people she looked to be pregnant. To bury her together with a fetus violated clan laws stating that a mother and fetus should be buried separately. The sanction for violating such a law is clan infertility. Some of her family, therefore, felt that she should not be buried until it was certain that there was no fetus. The absence of a fetus was not ascertained because the Christians were persuaded to bury her immediately by a missionary who thought it disrespectful to operate on the corpse under the circumstances. The missionary did not understand the consequences if the hospital diagnosis were wrong. In the end, it was necessary to sacrifice a goat to the ancestors to appease their wrath and to obtain forgiveness. Fertility returned to the clan.

Padri, I do not feel there is any conflict between being a Christian and a diviner. People come to me for help, and I have special powers from the ancestral spirits to heal them. I am able to give them the medicines and support they need to overcome evil in their lives just as my uncle gave me medicines and support when I was dying. Long before the missionaries came, the diviners were the healers of the people; this healing ministry continues to the present day.

The conversation with John continued for a short while but did not seem to take any direction. There was not the same rapport as there had been with Riana. John was not as articulate as Riana, and he tended to answer questions simply without elaborating.

At the end I thanked John for his time and patience. Everybody said good-bye and went off in the darkness. People were talking quietly about what they had heard. I realized while talking to John how little I understood of the religious role of a diviner-witch doctor. I was so unfamiliar with things that the ordinary people take for granted. I did not even know what questions to ask. I wondered whether I could ever get a sense of what ministry must mean to a diviner.

The air was damp with dew and the village was quiet as I walked back with the chairperson to his home. Occasionally the flicker of small kerosene lamps was visible through the open doorways of the grass-roofed homes.

Several weeks later, two theological students came to visit me, principally for the sake of learning how to do field research. Maxima Airo, the chairperson of a local Christian community, had arranged to invite a diviner to her home who would be willing to talk to the students. On the appointed day, in the early afternoon, the three of us arrived at her homestead by motorcycle.

Maxima's homestead was no longer hedged as it had been prior to villagization in 1972. The open area in front of her home was bare of grass and had been swept clean. A couple of folding chairs were in the shade of a large tree at the right. On the left was a corral for cattle.

Maxima greeted all with excitement and obvious pleasure. Several other Christians had dropped by to say Hello. They too greeted one and all. Maxima ushered us into the home where we met a small, older man who sat quietly. His name was Onyando. Greetings were exchanged.

As the students began to talk to the man, it became evident that his fluency in the Kiswahili language was quite limited. Maxima and I continually intervened with translations into Kijaluo (the local language) and English to facilitate the conversations.

One of the students asked: "Is your healing power through medicines or through the power of God?" The diviner answered immediately that it was God's power that heals. Then the student asked: "How do you know what kind of medicines to give in the treatment of sick people?" He answered that it is through dreams that he learns of the sick who are on their way to see him and knows which medicines are appropriate. The medicines, he said, are made with plants, roots, leaves, and herbs.

Onyando did not give much information about divination and he seemed a bit distraught and uncomfortable with the situation and the questions. His eyes shifted back and forth. He had trouble understanding the Kiswahili of the students and would often respond in Kijaluo. The making of traditional medicines seemed to be his major preoccupation. I began to think that perhaps Onyando was not a diviner but an herbalist—a traditional druggist who makes various drugs and powders to ward off sickness and problems.

After an hour and a half, the students had run out of questions and were tired. There did not seem to be much more information that could be gathered. They began to thank the gentleman for his time. At this point I noticed that Onyando was wearing a heavy copper bracelet. I began to question him about it: "Mzee, what is the signification of the copper bracelet you are wearing?"

Onyando looked at me with a certain amount of disbelief as he replied.

ONYANDO: This bracelet is warding off the ancestral spirit who is trying to kill me. I would be dead if it were not for this protective charm. My deceased mother had been the medium of that spirit. It is now trying to take possession of me. It has been open warfare. At times I have been close to dying; it has been and is a very painful process. I have been under the tutelage of another diviner who is teaching me how to deal with this spirit. Often sacrifices are demanded to appease the spirit.

When I heard his answer, I realized that Onyando was an apprentice diviner and not just an herbalist. He was still in the process of trying to come to grips with the possessing spirit. I also realized how strange my question about the bracelet must have been to him. The wearing of such a charm is a common sign of an apprenticing diviner. Everybody else in the culture would know this instinctively. I woefully pondered how out of step with the workings of the culture the students and I must seem, not only to the diviner but also to the ordinary people.

Again it was clear that the man had experienced a great deal of anxiety and pain in the process of coming to grips with the spirit that was attempting to use him as a medium. This seemed to explain some of his restlessness and his distracted gestures and responses.

As we were leaving, the man asked for a gift. I refused, thinking that it would be the wrong thing to do and would set a precedent that would make it difficult to do future research without paying. This would complicate the gathering of open and honest information. Of course, I was relying on the goodwill engendered by my ability to speak the local language and by my Christian ministry to the people.

As we left on motorcycles, I looked back at the homestead. I saw Maxima giving the man a five-shilling note—a gift for his time and efforts. I had clearly made the wrong response to the diviner's request. Maxima was covering for my mistake.

In the debriefing after the interview, the students expressed surprise at how much there was to learn about the symbolic meaning of cultural items, such as the bracelet. They speculated that there must be hundreds of such symbols in the culture that could be learned only through time and effort. Likewise they realized how difficult it is to deal with cultural symbols, values, and ideas in a trade language like Kiswahili, since it does not have the religious and cultural vocabulary of the traditional languages. Also it was clear from this interview that diviners were people who have had powerful emotional experiences with ancestral spirits. This experience gives the diviners the right and the power to speak for the ancestral spirits.

The following month I made a trip to visit another diviner, Okech, in the village where the diviner John was living. I was accompanied by a lay missionary who had just finished a four-month course in Kiswahili, and now wished to practice her new language skills and to observe the people in their rural setting. On that particular day her project was to meet and talk with a diviner.

It was a beautiful morning as we made our way along the paths to the homestead of Okech. Okech was the diviner mentioned in the introduction to this book who had predicted that someone would fall and be injured on the way home. Once again we were accompanied by the chairperson of the Catholic church in the village. This was my second visit to Okech's homestead. The previous year I had tried to visit Okech with another language student but had found him absent. As we entered Okech's homestead, a young man in his early thirties, dressed in an old T-shirt and a pair of wornout shorts, came over to greet us. It was Okech; we were greeted warmly. Okech was hyperactive, talking rapidly and energetically, walking back and forth somewhat uncontrollably. His eyes had a vacant stare. There were a number of well-fed cattle in the yard milling about together with goats and sheep. The diviner was obviously on the point of taking them out to pasture as he had his staff in hand. Folding chairs were brought out of a hut and all were seated in the yard. Okech began talking:

OKECH: Padri, it is nice to see you here. I knew that a white man was coming today because that goat over there, dedicated to the spirit of a white man, broke wind at sunrise.

MISSIONARY: Is that right? But, if that is so, why didn't that goat inform you of my visit last year when I came with a friend but found you absent?

OKECH: But I did know of it. I knew you were coming, but that particular day there was no one to shepherd the livestock for me. And since you arrived in the afternoon, there was no way I could leave the cattle and return to greet you. However, I am happy to see you and your friends. Welcome to my homestead.

MISSIONARY: Okech, I have come with this student who is interested in learning about diviners and divination. She will be working in this culture for several years and wants to understand as much as she can in order to be more effective in dealing with the people. Would it be possible for you to demonstrate how you divine?

OKECH: Mzee, you have come at the wrong time; all the ancestral spirits are sleeping. Come back tomorrow at sunrise when they are fully awake and active. It is not an easy matter to wake up the spirits in the late morning.

MISSIONARY: Okech, I do not expect you to actually do any divination, only to demonstrate how you do it. We are only here for a short while, and it would be impossible for us to return tomorrow.

OKECH: But one does not demonstrate or play at divination. It would offend the ancestral spirits to do so. You know, I have three ancestral spirits that speak through me. The first is the spirit of the founder of the Luo people, Ramogi, the second a female spirit from the Ganda people of Uganda, and the third a Maasai spirit. To wake them up without cause could make them angry, and to what purpose?

MISSIONARY: But can you not just demonstrate the ritual? There is no need to actually call on the spirits. Just do the rituals that you perform when you divine.

It was only after a prolonged conversation that the diviner agreed to show the ritual of divination—but reluctantly and with reservation. Afterward I realized that he had agreed only because he thought that the woman was asking for help.

Okech went into a small, circular hut nearby and brought out a gourd, a piece of dried animal skin about a foot square, and a canister that at one time had been the case of a quart thermos bottle. He laid the skin on the ground and began to shake the gourd with a slow, circular motion. The sound was enervating. He explained that this was the way of attracting the attention of the spirits. He then began to shake the canister and pour out the contents on the skin. The items were old coins, small seashells, and the dried head of a small bird. Okech gazed at them and pushed them around.

OKECH: My brother, as I told you the spirits are sleeping; they are silent; there are no messages.

MISSIONARY: But what are the meanings of the different items on the skin?

OKECH: The seashells are the spirits of the ancestors and the coins are the court guards. You see, the spirits are like kings and queens. They have guards, just like your kings and queens. Let me try to call them again. Ah, they are waking. Yes, the daughter of a white man is okay. She has no problems. There is nothing wrong with her.

As Okech spoke, I translated what he said into English for the woman. On the third roll of the "dice," Okech paused and then spoke.

OKECH: Wait a minute, there is something "short" about this white girl. At times she feels coldness coming over her.

This news electrified the young woman. "Ask him," she cried anxiously, "what he wants me to do to be cured." It seems that the woman had been in pain for twenty years with a little-understood circulatory problem called Raynaud's Phenomenon. Cold weather of any kind would turn her hands and feet blue and cause the pain of frostbite in the fingers and toes. I asked Okech what he wanted her to do.

OKECH: Tell her to come back in the morning at sunrise with a cow and I shall divine the cure.

After the demonstration Okech led us all to the small hut where he stored all his paraphernalia. There were rows of small pots filled with ashes made from various medicinal roots and plants. There were large bells, a dried monkey fist, a monkey-skin hat, a leopard skin, a variety of drums, and a collection of small canoes and wooden dishes. The dishes were for feeding the spirits, and the canoes were for their travel back and forth from Lake Victoria twenty miles away. The ancestral spirits are often said to live in the lake. The hut with all its medicines appeared to me to be something like a village pharmacy.

It was obvious that Okech was anxious to take his livestock out to pasture, and I began to thank him for his time and help.

OKECH: I am very glad, Mzee Padri, to show you and your friends how divination is done. Why don't you come back with your cameras and tape recorders, and I shall show you and teach you all the rites and rituals. It would be good for your people to understand and learn this ancient wisdom. It is the ordinary way of health and healing for our people. It ensures that the ancestral spirits are respected and obeyed.

MISSIONARY: I appreciate very much your interest and help. If I get the opportunity, I shall return and learn more about divination.

OKECH: If you decide to come back, I shall always know ahead of time. That goat never fails to alert me when a white man is coming. And you, my daughter, come back at sunrise with a cow and I shall work out your cure.

As we walked away, the young woman was almost hysterical. "Where can I get a cow?" she asked.

"For what?" I replied.

"In order to pay for my cure. That man can cure me. He understood my problem. I know he can do it."

"You are not serious, are you?" I answered.

"Of course I am," she said. "You don't think that this has happened by accident? I have been in pain for twenty years with this problem, and I know that this man has the power to make me well."

"This is only divination," I replied. "Surely you do not believe in that, do you?"

"I don't care what it is," she cried. "If he can cure me, then I am ready to pay the price. Get me a cow!"

When I saw that she was serious about seeking a cure through the diviner's mediation, I asked the local Christian chairperson what he thought the woman should do. Should she get a cow and return in the morning, or forget about it?

"This is a delicate matter, Padri," replied the chairperson. "It would look strange if this foreign woman, a leader of the church, should seek a cure from a diviner after all the negative things taught about diviners by the Christians. Whether or not he could help her is hard to say. However, I think it might be worth her while to try the cure if she could arrange it in some private way."

After much discussion, it was decided that it would not be in the best interest of either the woman or the local church to consult the diviner further. However, to this day the woman believes that the diviner could have cured her. Through this experience I began to realize that the phenomenon of divination was much more complex than I had previously thought. It appeared to me that the diviner was, in fact, communicating psychically with the spirit world. Otherwise, how would he have known of the woman's problem? Perhaps, I thought, even though the diviner explained his power in terms of ancestral spirits of which he is the spokesman, his skill is really the ability to read people's minds, and that is how he came to know of her problem. However, this theory may also be wrong, for the woman with Raynaud's Phenomenon claimed that this disorder was the furthest thing from her mind when speaking with the diviner. Furthermore, it was 100 degrees F. in the shade the day she met the diviner, and there were no visible signs of the problem.

Several weeks later, with all these experiences and thoughts about divination and diviners in the back of my mind, I made a special trip to visit my friend Riana and share what I had learned. It was my first trip back to Riana's homestead. When I arrived I was greeted happily by the widow Lucia. She quickly produced a folding chair from one of the huts and set it up under the shady overhang of the grass roof. "Karibu kiti, Padri" (Welcome, Padri, and please be seated), she exclaimed. At that point she sent one of the children to call Riana, who was out drinking beer at the homestead of one of the nearby neighbors. In about ten minutes Riana arrived. There was a broad smile on his face. He was happy to see me. After greetings, I started off the conversation.

MISSIONARY: Riana, I have been thinking about you the last month as I have been visiting several different diviners. They have been telling me about their lives and how they became mediums of ancestral spirits. One of them, Okech, even showed me how he divines by using various types of "dice." It was all very interesting. Now I am wondering if you, too, have had the same experience and training in becoming a diviner?

With that prompting, it was very easy to get Riana to tell of the events that led to his vocation as a diviner. His story was more or less a repeat of the stories of the other three diviners. He too had been critically ill, and through the mediation of a diviner had come to realize that an ancestral spirit was trying to possess him and make him its medium. He apprenticed under that diviner until a symbiotic relationship had been established with the spirit that ensured his good health at the cost of mediumship. It had been a very painful time, full of anxiety, dreams, and frustrations. But he emerged with the power to communicate and interpret the desires of the ancestors to the living. He is seen by the people as one who has a special place between the living and the dead. His powers enable him to help those in trouble.

When he had finished his story, Riana asked me to explain, in turn, how I had got the power to be a Christian diviner. This is what I told him.

MISSIONARY: Riana, this is not the first time that I have been called a diviner. However, I never think of myself in that category even though there is a song that the Christians sing in which Jesus is called a diviner. At any rate, let me tell you the story of how a Christian becomes a Catholic priest, a religious leader of the community. In many ways it is very different from your story.

It is felt that the spirit of the great Kiteme, called the Holy Spirit by the Christians, gives certain young men the desire to serve the Christian community in a special way by dedicating their entire lives to the church. This inner desire is called a "vocation," a special calling. One's vocation grows out of the nurturing of that inner desire to serve the church totally in any work designated by the church leaders, called "bishops." Many of these young men experience the desire to work for the church when they are still very young, nine or ten years of age. Others feel this vocation later in life. As these desires grow, the person applies to a special school where he begins his training to become a priest of the Christian church.

As you know there are many such schools in Tanzania these days training young African men to become Catholic priests. A few years back African students were accepted who were only in the fourth grade. I know one African priest who left his home and began his seminary training when he was only ten years old.

During the years of training there are special teachers, called "spiritual directors," who meet with each individual to help him discern whether or not the inner calling is true and whether or not the individual is a fit candidate, spiritually and physically, to undertake the role of a priest. Many of the young men realize after a period of time that the role and life of a priest are not for them, and they leave the training course. Others persevere until the end when a Christian leader, a bishop, calls them forth, lays his hands on their heads, and ordains them to work as his assistants. This rite we call "ordination" or "holy orders."

The source of priestly power is seen in the laying on of hands and not in a mystical vision or spiritual trauma. This ritual, holy orders, is said to put an indelible mark on the spirit of a person, making him a priest forever. Through this ritual the priest is given the power to serve the church in an official capacity as teacher, healer of the sick, and ritual leader of the Christian community under the direction of a bishop—the chief of the Christian community in a particular area. At the same time this ritual is seen to separate the priests from all the other members of the Christian community. The priests are called "clergy." They wear distinctive dress when they perform the special rituals of the church and often outside these rituals.

The priests are seen by many Christians to be special mediators between God and human. In many ways the priests are like diviners as they officially interpret the will of God to the living through their preaching, their administration of special rituals, and their counseling. Moreover, they generally live apart from ordinary people, some in special institutions and some in special religious communities. Others, like myself, leave their own countries and offer their services to Christian churches around the world as missionaries.

The ritual power given to the priests is not seen as something that belongs to them personally. This power is a gift of God to the Christian community. The priests exercise this power in the name of the people. Moreover, the priest does not see himself as having any special power to interpret the will of God other than that which he has gained through his theological studies and his own spirituality—a power available to each and every Christian. The work of the priest is to minister to the needs of the Christian community, especially its needs for the special rites called "sacraments." Also, for the past eight hundred years, the Roman Catholic Church in the West has insisted that those who offer themselves to serve as priests agree not to marry, not to found a family. This regulation is clearly only a rule, for there are branches of the Catholic Church in Eastern Europe that permit their priests to marry.

The training of a priest takes many years. Some study as long as ten years after secondary school. The core of their religious training is four years of study about God and religion, called "theology." During this time they learn all about our sacred book, the Bible. They study the history of the church and how it developed. They are taught the meaning of morality, and how to distinguish good and evil. They read the writings of the contemporary teachers who are attempting to apply the Christian message to the daily lives of Christians. And they spend a great deal of time in prayer, asking for guidance in their life and work.

At the same time it is recognized that all Christians are priestly. All are called by virtue of their initiation into the Christian church through a rite called "baptism" to be mediators between God and people. All are called to preach, heal, and lead in the name of Christ through the power of the Holy Spirit of God. The ordained priests, by way of contrast, make nurturing of the Christian community their full-time public work. They are the paid, official workers of the church.

Several of the special rituals of the church, the sacraments, can be performed only by priests. They alone are the ones who can say Mass, the memorial feast of Jesus that is performed each Sunday; grant the forgiveness of God to sinners; and anoint the sick and dying. Likewise they are the usual ministers of the ritual of baptism and the official witnesses of marriages.

In terms of lifestyle, the priests and bishops of the Christian communities are said to be servants of the people. This, however, is hard to measure, seeing that they do not have responsibility for the immediate care of families, and their daily needs are taken care of by the contributions of the Christian community. Likewise there are many priests who do specialized work, such as teaching in seminaries or schools, development work to raise funds for missionary work, journalism, and administration of institutions or communities. Often they are not directly involved in pastoral work. This type of work is seen as an indirect way of promoting the life and vitality of the Christian community.

One of the dimensions of priesthood of the Roman Catholic Church, Riana, is that it is not open to women. If women feel the desire to serve the church on a full-time basis, they seek acceptance in a religious community where they will be trained to dedicate their lives to living out gospel values of poverty, chastity, and obedience for the sake of the Christian community. These women are called "Sisters." Some of them work and live in this area. They minister to the various needs of the Christian community as nurses, doctors, teachers, social workers, or pastoral workers, but they cannot be ordained as priests. Presently, however, some Christian women are seeking to be ordained and have officially asked the Roman Catholic and other Christian churches to change this teaching. This prohibition against women priests, to my mind, seems unnecessary. In many Christian communities the women outnumber the men, are more interested in religion, and are better religious leaders.

Well, Riana, I do not know if this helps you to understand the work and life of a priest of the Christian churches, but at least it is a start. There are many more things that could be added, but I would first like to hear your reactions.

At this point Lucia carried over a small table and set out a couple of cups for tea. Some bananas and a small dish of sugar were placed on it. Lucia poured the tea. She then made the sign of the cross and said the blessing before food. Riana sat listening prayerfully. There were a few small children who had gathered around to listen to the conversation. No other adults were present as it was early in the afternoon and they were busy with their various daily chores.

Riana gave some of the bananas to the children. They were delighted.

RIANA: Mzee, I have always found it interesting that the young priests in this area are called "elders" by the Christians even though they are too young and inexperienced to deserve that title. Now, after hearing your explanation of the Christian priesthood, I understand why there is that confusion. The priests were made elders by virtue of their initiation rite into the priesthood. The same is true for our young men when they are circumcised. After the circumcision ritual they are considered adults capable of marriage and leadership in the community even though they are still untried and under the guidance of the older men. However, it seems that the Catholic priests, since they do not marry and take responsibility for a family, never really grow up. The failure to share one's life through procreation is interpreted by us as a tragic refusal to take full responsibility for the great gift of life given through Kiteme, the creator God. An unmarried person in this society is seen as unstable, disturbed, and not fully mature. So how can the unmarried state of the priest be a positive force in his role as a mediator between the ancestral spirits and humankind? Celibacy would make sense only if it were due to the demands of some ancestral spirit—the price one pays for the power of becoming a medium of that spirit—or if it were a necessary requirement for the efficacious performance of a ritual such as the traditional sacrifice of a cow to the ancestors. Otherwise it leaves the Christian priest in the permanent state of being an immature adult without responsibilities. There are no other unmarried adults in this society. What can be the meaning of your custom for Africans? What does such a custom do to a young man from our culture who believes he has a vocation to be a priest?

MISSIONARY: Riana, you have asked a question that has many dimensions regarding the life of a Christian priest. The rule of celibacy is clearly only a rule of the Roman Catholic Church. It is not believed to be a law coming from our God; therefore it is not demanded by our Christian faith. At the same time it is a rule that is not easily explained. For many of our teachers, the rule of celibacy is rooted in imitation of Jesus Christ. Jesus Christ was not married;

therefore the priest who seeks to be like Christ as closely as possible is not married. This seems to be the basis of the custom. At the same time, from the practical point of view of missionary work, people with family responsibilities usually are not able to live for long periods of time in foreign societies like your own as the celibate missionaries do. Likewise, the celibate missionaries are much more dependent psychologically on the local people for emotional and social support because they do not have intimate family relationships supporting them. They cannot "go home" to their families and close their doors to the African world. This tends to make them more sympathetic with the local culture.

However, these difficulties are not insurmountable. A few Protestant missionaries serve the African church together with their families for extended periods of time. Through their example of family life, their witness may be even stronger and more profound than that of the family-less Catholic missionaries.

Other Christian teachers feel that the historical roots of celibacy are not religious at all. They think that it arose out of a Greek idea that the body was matter and therefore evil, and procreation demeaning. As a consequence of this idea, married priests of the Greek religion when offering traditional sacrifices had to abstain from conjugal relations with their wives in order to be ritually pure—the very thing you just mentioned about African sacrifices. The Christian church seems to have accepted this notion of ritual purity without questioning its non-Christian roots. As early as the third century, there were calls for the celibacy of the priests. However, in the early days of the church most of the priests were married. The rule of celibacy was finally enforced in the Roman Catholic Church in the West eight hundred years ago. It was never enforced in the Eastern Catholic Church.

Some historians have recently argued that one of the most important effects of the celibacy of the clergy has been to keep the wealth and property of the church from being fragmented through inheritance and distribution to sons.

As to what celibacy means to the African priests and the communities they serve is hard to say. Does it leave the African priests in a category of immature and irresponsible men, or does it give them special influence and status as the Christians understand the sacrifice that they are making for the sake of the gospel? Only the Christians can answer that question.

As you see, Riana, there is no simple answer to the question of celibacy any more than there is a simple answer to your idea that the power to speak for the ancestors is due to a special mystical experience or contact with the dead. How are we to know if this mystical experience is no more than mental illness, called forth by some divine madness? In my society, people who claim such powers are usually considered mentally deranged and some are even placed in institutions for their own protection. What proof do you have that you are actually in contact with the ancestors? How do you know that your powers are derived from the influence and will of the ancestors rather than from your own skillful manipulation of the fears and ideas that motivate people?

RIANA: Padri, I am finding it difficult to understand your question. You know, of course, that there are people in our society who are mentally deranged and are known and treated as such. There is no problem distinguishing behavior caused by mental illness and behavior caused by the mediumship of ancestral spirits. The diviners and the mentally ill are clearly distinct. The mentally ill are not mediums of ancestral spirits. In fact one of the works of a diviner is to cure the mentally ill. Often the mentally ill are possessed by a bad ancestral spirit with whom the diviner communicates by means of a special language. He discovers what the possessing spirit wants and then provides the cure. Likewise, the fact that cures do take place under the invocation of the ancestral spirits is a clear sign that the ancestral spirits are at work. So, Mzee, it is the healing of people mentally, spiritually, and physically that has given and continues to give the diviners their position and power. Is there any other better explanation?

At the same time, Padri, many people see you missionaries as diviners of the Christian religion. They say that you divine with a book the way we divine with dice. Also, you have a secret language, special dress, and many rituals. The ritual you call baptism is believed to keep babies from dying. Indeed, in baptism are not Christian babies named after Christian ancestors the way non-Christian babies are named after clan ancestors? Another ritual, done over those critically ill, is said to help them die. Also, you are always calling on the Christian ancestors for help and guidance. You even say that your founder, Jesus, came back from the dead and showed himself to many people. Isn't this proof that you also believe in the power of ancestral spirits and the ability to communicate with them? I have heard Christian people say that they are possessed by the spirit of Christ. Is this not the same as saying that they are possessed by the spirits of the ancestors?

And, Mzee, why do you think the people give you so much respect? They think you are the powerful diviners of the Christian religion! But now you tell me that you do not have any special mystical powers, that you are merely a servant of the community where you live. This does not make sense, seeing the way you live without family, without roots, and far from your clan. Only a possessed person, the medium of a spirit, would be willing to live in such an isolated and, to my way of thinking, inhuman way and be happy with such a lifestyle. So why do you find it strange that people would see you as diviners like me, men with powerful mystical experiences, mediums of the Christian spirits? Are you not, in fact, Christian diviners?

MISSIONARY: Riana, we are *not* diviners. We are trained religious leaders offering our services to the Christian community. Divination is not part of our work. We do not even understand it. However, I realize now that some of the things we do must appear to be the actions and gestures of a diviner in an African culture. For example, recently I was accused in court by the chairperson of a neighboring village that I had burned down his house with lightning. When the police officer questioned me, I told him, somewhat in jest, that I was in Nairobi four hundred miles away when the house burned down, and I could not possibly have been the one responsible. When I realized, however, that the officer was taking the accusation seriously, I quickly said: "No, I didn't throw lightning at his house because I don't know how to do it."

It seemed that the people had been warning the chairperson of the village to be very careful with me because of my special powers, especially since we were having a dispute over the ownership and use of a building. Thus, when his house burned down, the chairperson felt it was a sure sign that my special powers were at work.

Although we are not diviners, we do say that we try to be of the same spirit and mind as Christ. We want to be like him before the Christian community. In this way one might say that we are mediums of Christ. We attempt to make his words and truth meaningful and present to the living. However, each and every Christian is called to this same ministry, not just the Christian priests. Also, there are in the Western Christian church special groups of Christians, called "charismatics," who pray over one another and cure one another in much the same way as African diviners. However, we attribute their success in healing to their faith in the power of God. So, Riana, you are right, there are rituals and prayers in our Christian traditions that are similar to the prayers and rituals of divination. Your rituals are in tune with the spirits of the ancestors; ours with the spirit of Jesus.

However, Riana, I still believe that your mediumship of the ancestral spirits is a psychological hoax. You pretend that you are in communion with a particular spirit, whereas in fact you are merely duping credulous people. You change your voice to a high pitch to make people think that it is a spirit talking. It is only you talking. You pretend to know the future, but what you say is so general that it could apply to just about anything or anybody. It seems to me that you are just play-acting. Your imagination is the source of all that is said and done. You publicize your own imagination and dreams, and not the will and desires of the ancestral spirits.

RIANA: Mzee Padri, it is very difficult to describe the way a spirit can take possession of you if you have never experienced it before. You often lose your own consciousness and become the very spirit that has taken control of you. How could a diviner fake such an experience? To do so would be to risk the anger of the ancestral spirits. It could lead to your death, the very thing that you struggled to avoid when you became an apprentice diviner. Mzee, this is not play-acting. It is a very serious business and not to be laughed at or scorned. If we were merely pretenders, we would be jeopardizing the very vitality and life of the community that we are called to protect and promote. Of course people are afraid of us. We are closer to the ancestral spirits than they. And yet, are not the Christian people afraid of you because of your close association with the things of God? Diviners are the spiritual leaders of the people. They stand between the living and the ancestral spirits, just as you priests stand between your Christian God and the Christian people.

Padri, this leads me to another question that seems to prove that you are, in fact, a practicing diviner. That is the question of your wealth. How are you able to live like a wealthy man even though you are without gardens and cattle? How can you afford to own and drive a car, a motorcycle, to hire a cook and housekeeper and live in a permanent house when you have no ordinary work? What is the source of your wealth? Do you get rich through divination? Do the people pay you with food and money when you cure them or do your rites for them—I have heard that one can pay twenty shillings to have a Mass said for one's special intention. Who is paying for all your things?

MISSIONARY: Riana, I know it may sound strange to you, but missionaries do not consider themselves wealthy. Our money comes from Christians in other parts of the world who want to help the Christian churches in Africa grow. Every month they send a certain amount of money for our living expenses. This helps pay for our food, cook, and maintenance of a car and motorcycle. We also receive money from the local parish council that goes toward our expenses. We are trying to encourage the community to increase their support each year so that, in the future, the total support for a priest working in the parish will be paid by the people. This way, when a local African priest is assigned to the parish, he will have enough income to support himself and his work. Our attitude toward all the things we have is that they are to be used for the good of the people. We could, of course, live a lot simpler, but like people all over the world, we seek a level of comfort with which we are familiar, and it is very hard for us to change our cultural habits. My own feeling is that the way we live is not as important to the people as is our sympathy and understanding of their needs and aspirations, and our willingness to share our things. I recall the Christians in a small nearby town saying how selfish one of the missionaries was because he sold his car to avoid being bothered by people who needed transportation.

However, even though we do have a lot of things, we are poor in terms of family. We have no sons to carry on our names, or wives and children to bring joy and life into our homes. These things we give up for the sake of our vocations, for the sake of the Christian church.

Riana, I have time for just this one last question as I must get back to the mission for an afternoon meeting. Often the cures you prescribe and the charms you make do not work. Does this not show that your healing powers are at best partial and often ineffective, that a person has just as good a chance at obtaining health without your ministrations? In other words, healing through divination is only by chance or good luck. You have no real power to consult the spirits to determine their will. All that you do or say merely makes the supplicant feel good about the problem. Furthermore, any results obtained are always interpreted in a positive light, even if a person dies. Divination is what we call "placebo" medicine, that is, medicine without any real power to cure.

RIANA: Mzee, you know it is very difficult to answer such a question, since you are again denying the very reality of divination and the mediumship of the diviner. However, to say that divination has no power to cure and to help those in need is contrary to our experience. Indeed, there are times when a cure does not take place, but this can usually be traced to the bad disposition of the ones involved, or to more powerful medicines being prepared by other diviners. At the same time, are your doctors with all their medicines and machines any more effective than ours? Do they always obtain a cure? Of course not. We are dealing here with the power of Kiteme, the creator, to heal, and this power never fails if properly applied. Do not belittle the power of Kiteme and the ancestors concerning the health and welfare of the living. Many people go to your mission hospitals and are not cured. They are then brought to a diviner and many recover.

I also have a final question for you, Padri. Why do you missionaries separate the people into various communities and cause dissention and friction among the people? The Seventh-Day Adventists first came to this area, saying that all should believe in Jesus and give up all traditional rituals and sacrifices. A short time later the Mennonites arrived and they proclaimed that *they* had Jesus, and not the Seventh-Day Adventists, and that people should convert to their way of thinking. Then the Anglicans arrived and said that *they* had Jesus, and finally the Catholics arrived with the same message. Now I am just an ordinary rural person without education. How am I supposed to sort out the conflicting claims of these various groups? What I do know is that someone is lying; you cannot all have the same truth about Jesus.

Yet you all preach that your Jesus wanted one big family, that he wanted his message proclaimed to all. However, do you not see that your various versions of Christianity create divisions and friction within families, clans, communities, and even nations—divisions and frictions that did not exist prior to your coming? I have even heard it said that missionaries will help you only if you belong to their denomination.

My work of divination, by way of contrast, is for the whole community. I do not distinguish people. Even you, Mzee, could come for healing and advice and not be turned away. Can you say the same if I came to you for one of your special rites? Christianity, Padri, has divided the people in this area, people who were naturally united.

MISSIONARY: Riana, what you say is absolutely true. Christianity has divided the African people even though it preaches a message of unity and brotherhood for all. This is a sad state of affairs. Instead of bringing many people closer together, it has sometimes pulled them apart. On the other hand, it has helped people of various clans who were traditionally hostile to one another to pray and meet together. However, often this show of unity is more superficial than real. Recently two clans of the Kuria people began a war over cattle thieving. The church building was in the territory of one of the clans. The Christians of the other clan were afraid to go to church for fear of being attacked. The faith of the Christians from the two clans was not strong enough to override traditional hostility and guarantee each other's personal safety.

Likewise, relief goods are often distributed in favor of a particular denomination even though the Western people giving the goods intend them for the whole community regardless of religious denomination. Last year, for example, wheat was shipped in by the Mennonite church in response to a famine. It was given to the local Mennonite pastors, who distributed it only to their own congregations. The Catholic Relief Services, an international relief organization, sends bales of used clothing to the Catholic mission stations. Often these clothes go only to the Catholics even though they are intended for the whole community. One church leader, an

African, was reported to be using these clothes to pay workers who were building for him. Another, a missionary, claims that he paid for small chapels in various villages through the sale of these clothes. It almost seems as if the traditional African societies together with governmental and world organizations are more ecumenical and just than the Christian churches in the distribution of relief goods.

However, things are not all that simple. Recently the women in my parish formed a women's co-op. They excluded the non-Catholic women of the villages, arguing that the source of their unity was their Catholic faith. Without this bond, they said, it would be very difficult to get the loyal cooperation of the other women. Previous attempts to form a co-op with the entire population of women were cited as proof of their argument.

Also, Riana, as you supposed, my church would not allow me to give you one of our special rites. These rites are reserved only for the Christian believers who are without serious sins in their lives. Is this discrimination? Is this a perversion of the Christian message? Could you imagine Jesus refusing to help someone, bless someone, forgive someone because the person did not fit into a certain category of believers? This divisiveness of Christianity in Africa is a whole area of confusion, pain, and suffering that needs to be addressed and treated. The sooner the better. Western missionaries as a group, you know, are very conservative people theologically and politically. They tend to accept things as they are and fail to see and address the injustices present in their work. They read the fragmentation of their own Western societies into the African scene and assume that the unity proclaimed by Christianity is something new and unique in the lives of the local people—a misjudgment if there ever was one.

Well, Riana, this has certainly been an interesting discussion, since you have just about convinced me that we are both diviners—you of the traditional religion and I of the Christian religion. We have much more in common through our role and work in the society than I had previously realized. You have made me more aware of how people relate to me as a diviner and also how the Christian denominations are destructive of traditional unity.

However, Riana, many missionaries would not accept the label "diviner" even though many things they do and say indicate that they have special mystical powers. For example, I remember a missionary once saying Mass for the repentance of thieves who had stolen church property. The next day the property was returned. Again, I recall a missionary expelling an African man from the church by means of a special rite called "excommunication." The man drowned three days later in Lake Victoria—an obvious sign to the people of the missionary's mystical powers.

With that final example, the conversation ended. I was tired and wished to head back to the mission for a meeting, and Riana wanted to go back to the beer party. I arose, shook hands with Riana, and then said good-bye to Lucia and the children. Lucia gave me two fresh eggs, which I carefully wrapped in a handkerchief and placed in my jacket pocket. I put on my leather gloves and cap, mounted the motorcycle, and drove slowly out of the homestead. As usual, several children tagged along for a short distance.

COMMENTARY

In this discussion it is again clear that the worldviews are the controlling factor in the way religious leadership is structured. For Riana, with his one-world view, it is the ancestors who hold the key to health, prosperity, and the good life. The problem, of course, is how to contact them so as to know their wills and desires. This is where the diviner fits in. He is the "Jesus" figure of the traditional religion, able to communicate back and forth between the dead and the living. He is a person seemingly chosen at random by the ancestors to become their spokesperson. Likewise, as we hear in the dialogue, the call of the ancestors is very dangerous, dramatic, and painful. All four diviners spoke of the life-threatening dimension of their apprenticeship, and the "cost" entailed in becoming a diviner. The end result is that they can appeal to that experience as the source of their power and ability to speak for the dead.

Western Christianity, on the other hand, preaches a two-world view of reality: this imperfect world and the new world promised to those who are saved. However, there seems to be an infinite chasm between these two worlds—the chasm of divinity vs. humanity, and creator vs. creature. Only a cosmic person can bridge that gap; a mere human being cannot. For the Christian that cosmic person is

Jesus Christ, who is both God and human. There can be no other mediator. No human person can do what he does. Therefore, the root of the Christian priestly ministry is service to the Christian community in order to keep it in touch with its cosmic leader, Jesus, through the special rituals of the sacraments. The Christian priest is not divinely chosen through a powerful mystical experience to do this work full-time; rather, he offers himself in response to an inner calling. There is no suggestion that the priest is divinely possessed so as to have a special mystical status within the community. The priests of Christianity are basically servants and functionaries of the Christian communities.

In the case of the clerical Catholic priesthood, there is a certain ambivalence. The things that distinguish the Catholic priest from the people, with the exception of the sacramental activity, are cultural and arbitrary—clerical celibacy, special dress, training, and lifestyle. Furthermore, it often seems that these external elements of priestly life can be more of a hindrance than a help in giving service to the Christian community.

The question raised by Riana about the conflict experienced by the African clergy in terms of celibacy is very important. The commitment not to marry and found a family must truly be extraordinary given their traditional worldview. It seems to me that the choice of an African priest for celibacy entails a choice to remain a perpetual adolescent in the eyes of the elders of the society—a demand not made on Western priests, where their societies do not evaluate maturity in the same manner.

Likewise the lifestyle and role of the clerical Christian priest in the traditional society is brand-new. There was never such a figure in the society prior to the advent of Christianity. This is again an instance of how the Christian churches merely imposed their structures on the African church. Later on, many of the independent Christian churches broke with their founding churches over the issue of religious leadership and clerical lifestyle.

The orientation of the diviners to the healing of all evils is dramatic. They are the ones who facilitate the smooth order in the society. Their main preoccupation is to help those who have fallen on evil times. As a young Christian missionary, on the other hand, I tended to treat most physical and mental illnesses scientifically. I did not see those illnesses as central to my ministry. But what is central to Christian ministry? Is it the confecting of the sacraments for the Christians in order to link them to Christ at special occasions in their lives? It appears to me that this is the main apostolate for many missionaries. They link the faithful Christian people to the cosmic person of Jesus through sacraments of salvation in the way that Riana links the people to the ancestors to obtain reconciliation and relief.

In retrospect, the African people had to understand the Christian priests as diviners. There was no other role or model into which the Christian priest could fit. A great deal of the respect and interest of the people in the Christian priesthood, no doubt, came from this linkage. The more a Christian priest takes on the role of the diviner—the divinely inspired healer—the more effective and meaningful he becomes in the lives of the Africans. The fact that the African Christians can find nothing wrong with calling Jesus a diviner, in song, is a clue that the kind of religious leadership that the people know, want, and understand is that provided by diviners.

5

Everlasting Life: Remembrance or Resurrection

Early one morning a plaintive wail rose and spread throughout Ingri village. Someone had just died. I turned over in bed wondering who it might have been. I got up and looked out the window to see where the wailing was coming from, but it was still too dark and only the general direction could be determined. It was probably Odhiambo, I thought, an old man who had been critically ill for several weeks. He had asked to be baptized even though he had several wives. One of the catechists had baptized him with the understanding that, if he recovered, he would straighten out his marriage affairs according to the laws of the church. Now, it seemed, God had called him.

About 11:00 A.M. one of the Christian members of Odhiambo's family came and called me to conduct the burial rites. Together we set out for a nearby homestead. There I found a large group of neighbors and relatives. The grave had already been dug, and the corpse was in one of the houses, lying on a skin made from the hide of a bull—Luo people are born and die on such skins. The corpse had been sewn into a body bag made from white muslin cloth—a recent addition to the funeral rituals in imitation of Muslim customs.

The time had come for the burial and the corpse was carried to the edge of the grave. I opened my prayer book and began to recite the prayers for the dead. The people responded where possible. I gave a short homily about the Christian hope in the resurrection of the dead. Several people offered special prayers, saying: "Let our brother be at peace." "May he see the ancestors." "May he be blessed with everlasting life." "May his sins be forgiven."

The grave and the corpse were then blessed with holy water and the sign of the cross. The Christians began to sing as two young men climbed into the grave to receive the corpse as it was lowered. Once the corpse had been properly positioned on its side and the young men had climbed back out of the grave, I threw a handful of dirt down onto the corpse, as did the other mourners. Then the young men began, with shovels, to fill in the grave. A long hollow reed was placed near the ear of the corpse and held in position as the grave was being filled. This would enable a diviner to communicate directly with the deceased later on. Once the grave had been filled, rocks were placed on it to keep it from being dug up by animals, and a simple wooden cross was stuck into the ground at one end. The reed protruded about six inches from the top of the grave. The death wail began again. "Whoo lolo ree, whoo lolo ree, whoo lolo ree, whoo lolo ree," they cried. "Our brother is gone! Our brother is gone! Our brother is lost." Some of the wives of the deceased took pieces of his clothing and ran back and forth wailing and crying, shaking the clothing in the air.

Along the road and pathways leading to the village, relatives and friends of the deceased could be seen coming to pay their last respects. As each group drew close, they would begin the funeral wail in earnest.

An awning was being hastily constructed, with poles stuck into the ground and tied together with thin saplings and then covered with green branches. The structure was temporary but served the purpose of giving shade. Large quantities of food were being prepared for the guests by the women. Their work centered around several three-stone fireplaces where large clay pots had been placed for cooking stiff porridge and meat. Some of the younger girls were setting out to fetch water from a nearby stream. An empty forty-four-gallon oil drum had been borrowed from a neighbor to hold the extra water. Just outside the homestead, a cow was being butchered by the men to provide meat. There was a certain order and ritual in all the noise and confusion.

After sitting for a while and talking with some of the elders, I got up and started to return home. I had noticed that a pickup truck had turned into the mission station, and I wanted to see who the visitor was. I promised the family that I would return for food—not to eat at a funeral would be seen as insulting to the family and indicate that the person had something to do with the death.

The visitor turned out to be one of my colleagues from a neighboring mission who was on his way to the post office thirty miles away. We sat and drank coffee for a half-hour or so while exchanging news. We arranged that he would return in the evening for supper and spend the night.

In mid-afternoon I returned to the funeral. As I entered the homestead of the deceased, I noticed Riana among the mourners— the dead person was the brother of one of Riana's wives. We greeted one another with special feelings of friendship. A chair was offered me next to Riana under the leafy awning. I began to converse with him.

MISSIONARY: Well, Riana, what a pleasant surprise. I have been thinking about you and all the things we have discussed. Your ideas have certainly helped me understand the religious mentality of the people.

RIANA: Padri, I was hoping that you would be here and we would have the chance to continue our discussion. Odhiambo's death and burial certainly furnishes a ready-made topic for debate. What do you think?

MISSIONARY: A great idea, Riana. As we sit here, I am wondering what the people really think has happened to Odhiambo. Where is he now that he has died? What does life mean to him now that his body is buried in a grave?

RIANA: Padri, it is very clear in our tradition that death is only the first stage in the process of dying. The deceased person is still alive and present to the living, for we can see his things, his wives, his children, his cattle. Physical death for us is merely the beginning of dying. This is the main reason why a widow is not seen as capable of remarriage, as we have already discussed. She continues to be married to her husband even though he has physically died. Likewise, as we have also discussed, we know that a person is still alive after death because he or she appears to us in dreams asking us for favors, or complaining about our behavior. And the thing that they most often request is that newborn babies be named after them. This ensures that the person lives on through their namesakes. In some real way we believe that these babies are in fact the ancestors returned, as they usually have the characteristics, manners, and temperament of those whose names they carry. The deceased, therefore, remain alive through remembrance and through the grandchildren who carry their names. This is so important that the ordinary person can tell you the names of his or her ancestors back to seven generations. These ancestors are known as the living dead. To forget the names of these ancestors would be to invite their anger. However, when an ancestor's name is finally forgotten, then the ancestor is said to be completely dead. He or she has now joined the company of the unknown ancestors. This is the reason why it is so important that a person have children. It is through one's children that one continues to live.

Another request that is often made by ancestors in dreams is that a feast be given in their memory. These feasts are quite common. They are called by some "tea parties." They are almost identical to a feast given to honor a living grandparent or parent. Large amounts of beer and food are prepared and a cow is set aside. Invitations go out to all the friends of the deceased. On the day of the feast, early in the morning, the cow is sacrificed in the name of the ancestor. As the party gets under way, there is drinking, dancing, eating, and singing. Sometimes these parties continue for several days. The deceased person is honored just as if he or she were alive.

While Riana was talking, a group of people driving cattle ahead of them burst into the homestead and ran the cattle over the grave. The men were dressed in their traditional battle array. They carried buffalo-hide shields and long spears, and wore headpieces made of monkey skins. Several carried high-pitched drums, which they beat with a hurried rhythm. One man blew a horn made of a large gourd, which gave the loud mourning sound heard only at funerals. They ran back and forth in the homestead in mock conflict with an imaginary enemy. At one point they came close to Riana and me, shaking their spears at our faces threateningly while dancing from side to side. Both of us smiled and greeted the warriors. After a short period the group moved out of the homestead, running the cattle in front of them. They were heading for a remote pasture land several miles away. Riana broke the silence.

RIANA: What you are seeing, Padri, is the way in which death is driven from the village. It is felt that a death is never accidental but has been caused by someone, either a witch or an angry ancestor. It is important that death itself be chased away so that no one else dies. That is why the warriors are searching for death and then driving it, along with the cattle, to a remote place where it will be isolated. Also, the bringing of the cattle to the funeral is a sign of respect for the deceased and honors that person's memory. However, the state of a person after death is only vaguely understood. We see the bones in the ground, so we know that the person no longer is like one who is living. That is, one does not have a mouth for eating or eyes for seeing or hands and arms for working. At the same time, though, we know that they can eat, for they often ask for an animal sacrifice, and food is offered to them. For example, while honoring such a request, we pray:

> We are bringing you a chicken. We are giving it to you, to eat with your brothers. We are also going to eat it together with you.

Also, at times, the sacrificer breaks off some of the meat of the sacrifice and goes outside the house and prays, throwing the meat from side to side:

> This is your sacrifice, you the spirits. Eat, one and all, the chicken we are giving you. Let our sick sister rise up. Grandmothers, grandfathers, call yourselves together. Come and eat with us, so that our sister will stand up.

The dead ancestors, as we have already discussed, are seen as the owners of the land and are clearly seen to have power over evil, at least the power to ameliorate it or to prevent it. When evil strikes, the ancestors are often divined to be unhappy with their offspring. There has been a breakdown in communication between the living and the dead. The solution is to reestablish contact with the ancestors. This is done through a sacrifice in which the dead ancestors are called once again to eat with the living, to forgive them, to be reconciled with them.

In some of our clans, when a person reaches a ripe old age, a special ceremony is performed that installs the person into a class of elders. One who has been installed seems to bridge the gap between this visible world and the spirit world, and to be placed in a state of particular intimacy with the ancestral spirits. Also, one who has gone through the elderhood ritual is believed by some to have ensured reincarnation in the life of a grandchild with the least possible delay. At the same time such a person is seen to be a living saint. This person is one who can be trusted with money and goods, one who cannot lie, cheat, or commit adultery. This person is an example of a wise, fully mature, and perfected human being.

You see, Mzee Padri, Kiteme created only one world wherein humankind lives, dies, and is reborn through names. However, if people die without children, no one will name their children after them. Such people quickly enter into the realm of the unknown ancestors where their names are lost forever. So it appears that the final state of a person depends on fertility. Those with children return to the state of human life as their own grandchildren. Those without progeny disappear into the community of the unknown ancestral spirits, called *Ebewe*.

All in all, we do believe there is life after death. In one case the dead return to the land of the living; in the other, the dead remain in the community of the ancestors. We pray at sacrifices:

> My grandfather, come to your feast that I am making for you. Call yourselves together. Bring all your brothers together—all you people who have gone to your rest, even those whose names we have forgotten.

From this perspective, life is a cyclic affair—a coming and going from this visible human life to the ancestral spirit life and then returning to this human life as grandchildren. Life, therefore, is a shared reality received from the ancestors and shared again with the ancestors. Each person is, in a sense, his or her own grandparent. Every baby born is given the name of a designated ancestor whose life he or she carries. And each baby is addressed by the elders as a particular grandparent, father, mother, son, or daughter. The living adults see their parents returning to this visible world in the lives of their children. At birth, a diviner gives the baby its ancestral spirit name. At that point it is considered to be a full member of the human community. If a baby is stillborn or dies shortly after birth before it is named, it is not considered to be a part of the human community and is not buried as a human being.

At this point a very old man and woman, steadying themselves with walking sticks, shuffled into the homestead. They gave out the mourners' wail as they approached the grave. "Woo loo loo rey, woo loo loo rey," they shouted. "Our brother is gone. Our brother is lost."

RIANA: Mzee, old people like these are obliged to come and pay their respects to the deceased even though, for many, it is very painful to walk. Not to do so could be a sign that they were somehow involved in the death, either directly through witchcraft or indirectly through bad feelings. By coming to the funeral, they show the community that they were in good relations with the deceased. This also ensures that they too will be properly buried upon their deaths, and they will be well received by those who have gone before them.

The ancestors, we believe, are close to Iryoba, and Nyamhanga, the intermediaries of Kiteme, and that is why they can mediate Kiteme's power and presence to the living. At times, in our prayers, we do not distinguish among Kiteme, his intermediaries, and the ancestors. We call on them together, saying:

Oh you our Father, God the Almighty, the Sun, accept us. You are our God. Accept this our sacrifice. Our ancestors, our forefathers, come—accept this sacrifice. . . . Yes, all-powerful God our protector, you our forefathers, you have accepted this our sacrifice. We are the evil ones. May you shine on us well. . . . All-present God, our Father, may the misfortune that is finishing us all go out of here. Yaye, our elders, our fathers, we are disappearing on earth. Help us one and all.

As you can see, Mzee, from these prayers, it is clear that Kiteme and the ancestors are concerned about the life and health of the living. This is further evidence that there is a life after death, and this life is under the power of the great Kiteme. It even seems that the ancestors become the mediators of the power of Kiteme over the living. They are given the task to watch over the living and ensure that all is kept in proper order. Their unhappiness and anger with the living causes them to suspend their protecting power and, as a result, evils begin to disturb the human community. The way to overcome the evil is reconciliation with the ancestors. We pray:

We are standing before you, yes, our ancestors. We are offering you a bull. We are coming so that you may help us. You drive away from us the evil thing that is destroying us, so that it goes out from us. Aa, owners of the land, rescue us all. Accept, one and all, this cow that we are giving you.

When an old person dies, great care is taken to bury him or her properly so that the person will not have bad will toward the living and use ancestral influence to allow evils to afflict the living. This is also the reason why elderly people in this society are given a great deal of respect. There is fear that, if one abuses an elderly person, after death that person will repay the offender with unmitigated problems such as sicknesses, bad luck, and even death itself. One must be on the good side of the elderly because they will shortly be joining the ancestors and participating in the distribution of Kiteme's saving power in the land of the living.

Unity with the ancestors is essential, Padri, if one is to live in peace and prosperity. The remembered ancestors, the living dead, are the essential stabilizing forces in our lives. We could not even live if it were not for their power, love, and protection. Human life for us, therefore, involves the unborn, the living, the living dead, and the unknown dead. It is like a circle: at the top are the unknown ancestors, at the bottom the living, at the right the recently dead, and on the left the unborn. We see each one of these stages as part of our life cycle as we share our lives with the next generation and then enter into the land of the ancestors. To forget one's ancestors is equivalent to forgetting one's children. This unity with the ancestral spirits is what gives human life its ultimate meaning.

Truly, Mzee, we are people of community, of lineage. Life for us is a gift, given to be shared. Not to share life through procreation is a sign that one is somehow damming up the life forces that give our community vitality. For such a one it is said that the door of his or her house has broken down, for there will be no one to remember that person after death. There will be no grandchild to carry on the name. Nominal reincarnation will be impossible. Such a person quickly becomes an unknown ancestor.

At this point a young girl brought water for the washing of hands. A large table was placed in front of us and a number of the elders gathered around. Large plates of stiff porridge were placed on the table along with dishes of stewed meat. After all had washed their hands, the young girl said the Christian prayer before meals. Then all began to eat eagerly. Conversation drifted about, dealing with the life of the deceased, local political matters, the weather. At the end of the meal, after all had again washed their hands and made themselves comfortable, I returned to the conversation with Riana.

MISSIONARY: Riana, I am surprised at how important the dead are to the living. This is certainly not true in my tradition. When someone dies in my society, he or she is seen as being severed from the living legally, economically, and socially. This is why a woman, as we have seen, can remarry after the death of her husband—death ends marriages. However, let me tell you how the people in my culture deal with and understand death and dying.

First of all, many people in the Western world do not respect the elderly as you do. We seem to feel that old age is a time of waiting for death. Most of the elderly live by themselves or with older people in institutions, old folks homes, or hospitals until death. Most of the elderly do not even want to be cared for by their children because they feel that they would be a burden.

Our belief is that life comes only from God, and God alone has the right to take it back. At the conception of a baby, a new, unique human life is created by God, which will exist forever either in glory with the saved or in misery with the damned. At the point of death, it is God who calls the person to account for his or her deeds. No one has the right to take another's life. Nor does an individual have any right to commit suicide. It is often said that an elderly person who is spared a long and painful illness by dying suddenly is blessed by God. At the point of death, we believe that the soul or spirit of the person leaves the body and goes to God. The body is left behind like a shell, its usefulness finished.

After a person has died, a special company is called to take the body and prepare it for burial. Usually this preparation involves the draining of the blood from the body and the injection of a preservative fluid to keep the body from decaying for several days. Then the body is dressed in new clothes and laid out in a box as if the person were sleeping. Some of these boxes are made of wood, others of metal. If the family selects a metal box, the cost can be very high. The body is then displayed in a room provided by the burial company for a period of usually two or three days so that friends and family can view the body. During this time the family tends to talk and act as if the person were still alive. This ritual allows the living to accept the fact that the person has indeed died.

All the family, friends, and relatives of the deceased gather at the funeral room to pay their last respects. Many of the relatives and close friends offer gifts of flowers; others give contributions to special charitable organizations in the name of the dead person.

In the case of a Catholic Christian, many arrange to have a memorial Mass said for the deceased. Likewise, the evening before the burial, there is usually a prayer service. Then, on the day of the funeral, the body is escorted to the church and placed before the altar. A funeral Mass is said for the deceased and the body is blessed with holy water. People are seated in the church according to their relationship with the deceased—the closer the relationship, the closer one sits to the box containing the corpse. This same ordering of people is followed in the funeral procession from the church to the place of burial.

In our tradition, the bodies of all the deceased are buried in special places called graveyards. At the time of burial the box containing the body is usually lowered into another, bigger box made of concrete. The second box is then sealed so that no water or air can get to the body. The grave is then covered over. Several months later a marker made of stone or metal, inscribed with the person's name and date of birth and death, is placed on top of the grave.

After the rites at the graveyard, all the participants are invited to a designated place for food and drink. Often the food has been prepared by a church group or by friends of the family. At the end of the meal, the funeral rites are finished. We are not like you Africans who continue the funeral for days on end.

Some time later, the last will and testament of the person is read, and his or her material goods are distributed according to that document. Sometimes, as I have said, certain members of a family are left with nothing—an irrevocable answer to unresolved personal conflicts.

When people die, we believe that they appear before the great creator God and are judged to be good or evil on the basis of their actions while living. Those who have loved and lived good lives are rewarded with the sight of God and are welcomed into the community of the saints in a place called "heaven." Those whose evil deeds declare them unfit to see God are thrown out of the heavenly court into the company of the devil and all evil persons who have lived and died since the beginning of time, in a place called "hell." There they will live forever in misery with no hope of ever changing their status. God, in our belief, does not play games with us. He takes us so seriously that we are able to turn away from him forever.

The saved people live in harmony, happiness, and peace. There is no longer any sickness, suffering, disease, or evil. God lives among them forever, as their Father. This is what the Christians call "everlasting life."

You see, Riana, in our belief, humanity is destined to live in a new world different from the one we see and live in at this period. This world is a temporary world, a world made imperfect by sin. This world will pass away, and a new world will take its place. This new world again is divided into two parts, the part where evil will no longer have any power over those who are holy, and the part where sinners will live in eternal damnation. Some of our great teachers say that the new world of the saved is in fact the primal world of our first parents, Adam and Eve. If so, this would mean that the faithful are returning to a world as it was originally created by God—the Garden of Eden, as our Holy Book symbolically describes it.

Finally, we believe that, at some point in the future, time will end and Jesus the Son of God will return in glory to judge publicly all creation. At that time the dead will rise with human bodies. The bodies of the saved will be restored in full glory and perfection—the crippled will no longer be crippled; the blind no longer blind. Each and every saved person will be the unique and perfect creation as intended by God when they were created. The bodies of the damned will also be resurrected, but for them it will be unto shame and misery.

Our Christian teachings, Riana, are very clear about the existence of an afterlife. A person never goes out of existence once created, and at some point after death one's body will be resurrected for better or for worse. Humanity is called to live like God in perfect harmony and perfection without limit or end. It almost seems as if humanity is called to become lesser gods under the power and goodness of the great God creator. And that is the final destiny and glory of humanity. There is no other reality. This is the Good News brought by our leader Jesus Christ: every person is called to sonship or daughtership with God the Father. To have lived and died without ever hearing this message, and believing it, has to be one of the greatest tragedies of life. Indeed, most of the new converts to the Catholic Church, as I have already pointed out, say that it was this message of everlasting life with God, above everything else, that attracted them to Christianity. The very idea of living on forever in glory with God in happiness is without doubt the most fantastic claim of Christianity. Unfortunately, however, one can freely reject that destiny forever.

On the other hand, once a person is dead, there is no belief that they have any direct power over the lives of the living. Of course, they live on in the memories of those who loved them, and prayers are often said for their safe passage to heaven—asking that God will have mercy on them and forgive them their sins. However, since no one has ever come back from the grave, no one knows for certain what awaits one in the afterlife. It seems, at least in the popular imagination, that the dead in our Christian tradition are in some kind of shadowy existence awaiting the resurrection. Most teachers, though, feel that the dead are already resurrected and live either in heaven with God or in hell with the devil. In the first case, however, the dead are seen to be at peace with God, where no evil of any kind can touch them—the reward for their loving and faithful service of God while living on this earth.

There are Christians, indeed, who will pray to the dead faithful ancestors for help in time of need, especially those ancestors who were seen to have exceptional holiness. The church has even officially declared that certain people have indeed reached heaven and are to be known as "saints." These saints are celebrated as the heroes of our religion. They are the ones who have fought against and overcome evil while living on this earth. Furthermore, the whole community of the saved are called the "communion of saints," and once a year there is a celebration in their honor. There are also special rituals set up to honor specific saints. For example, St. Anthony is celebrated as one who can help find a lost object; another, St. Jude, is called upon for help in hopeless cases. Moreover there is one saint, Mary, the mother of Jesus, who is seen to have special powers to intercede with Jesus in any kind of imaginable situation. She is the highest of saints and the closest to God. Some non-Catholics feel that the Catholic Christians worship Mary as a feminine type of God. This is not true. She is reverenced as the ancestor that accepted the will and power of God in her life more than any other living or deceased person. As a reward for her faithfulness, we believe that before her body decayed, God raised her up from the dead and she was taken into heaven body and soul. She was the first human being to receive complete salvation. She is seen as the prototype of what will happen to each and every person who is faithful to God's laws while alive on this earth.

At this point, another group of mourners burst into the homestead, shouting, crying, and wailing. They were from the family of the eldest daughter of the deceased. These people came with sheep and goats, which were to be contributed to the funeral costs. After five minutes or so of wailing, they began to quiet down and started to greet some of their friends. The older men moved over to the awning, looking for chairs, while the women offered their services in the preparation of food. Several of the people made a special point to greet Riana and me by shaking hands. Most of the other mourners went about their business without much notice of the new arrivals. Riana continued the conversation.

RIANA: Mzee, your burial customs and your ideas about the afterlife seem very strange to me. First of all, why do you drain the blood out of the body, and what do you do with the blood? Is it used for medicines? And why do you bury the body in two boxes? What is the meaning of such a custom? And what is the meaning of the flowers? What could a dead person do with such a gift?

MISSIONARY: Riana, the blood is replaced with a fluid that preserves the body from decaying for several days. There is no special meaning attached to the blood; I suppose it is merely poured out after the procedure. No medicine is made from it as far as I know. Practically, this preservation of the body allows the living to prepare the funeral and to send the news of the death to all concerned. However, there are some who feel that this ritual is an attempt to stop the process of death by keeping the body from decaying, making it immortal. The same would be true of the cement box. They would link this custom with the practice of the Egyptians who many centuries ago turned the bodies of the dead into stone. Others, however, feel that these customs, besides their practicality, serve to remind the living of the sacredness of the body, especially since it will be resurrected on the day of the final judgment.

At one time the Catholic Church forbade Christians to burn the bodies of the dead, for it was said that cremation was a sign of disbelief in the afterlife. These days, however, there does not seem to be the same concern about the body. Some people donate their bodies to hospitals for research, while others arrange to have their bodies burned immediately without being embalmed.

The flowers brought to funerals are seen by most as signs of beauty and new life, and their smell sweetens the air. Very few realize that they are a type of sacrificial offering—the destroying of something of value in the name of the deceased friend.

Riana, I have in turn a question for you. The thing I find most difficult to understand about your description of the afterlife is the idea that an ancestor returns to human life through an infant that carries his or her name. But what evidence do you have for such a teaching? How can life be recycled? How can anyone return from the dead in the guise of another, a child? For a Christian, death is the final event of life in this transitory world; there is no return to this world, to this kind of human existence. However, you seem to be saying that one returns to this world in an unending cycle until one is finally forgotten, and that this world is the only real, permanent, and true world, the only place to live and be human. This belief stands in opposition to the Christian belief that this world is a fading, temporary world leading to another new and permanent world, a world where humankind will live in fulfillment with God.

A year ago I met an anthropologist from Switzerland who was doing research on the idea of nominal reincarnation in the Musoma area. He said that it was very difficult to understand exactly what was meant and understood by nominal reincarnation. He had been unable to find anyone who was able to articulate clearly the reasoning behind this idea. He felt that it was definitely not a kind of Hindu reincarnation in which a person continues to be reborn in various human and nonhuman forms until reaching a stage of perfection that allows escape from this cycle. At the same time there did not seem to be any consistent answer to whether or not the new person was in fact the reborn ancestor.

Since then I have asked a number of people if they are the ancestors whose names they carry. Most reply that they have no conscious awareness of being those ancestors even though they are addressed by the elders as ancestors. For example, one young man said he is always greeted by his grandmother as her deceased husband and is treated as such. Another said that he is a particular ancestor because people have convinced him that he looks like that ancestor and has the same personality. Likewise, you often hear people comment on the behavior of an individual as an extension and continuation of the life and activity of the ancestor. They say, for example: "Of course he is generous. Listen to his name! He is that generous ancestor." But none of these explanations seems to be adequate. Riana, what is your explanation of African reincarnation?

RIANA: Padri, you are asking for an answer to a question that seems so obvious to us. We are the ancestors! How do we know this? Well, first of all our experience of living things points to the cycle of death and rebirth. For example, in the planting of the cassava branches, the old plant dies, but its shoots continue the original life of the plant. The planting of seeds illustrates the same lesson as cassava. The birth of our cattle, goats, and sheep with the same coloring and characteristics as the parents points to a sharing of the same life force. The birth of children with the same looks and bearing as their parents tells us that their life is a sharing in an existing life that is recycled through procreation. Life, given as a gift from the ancestors, is shared back with them through procreation. However, the major proof of this reality is that the ancestors appear to us at night while we are sleeping. They ask for things, talk to us, and even travel with us. They often ask for the sacrifice of a goat or a sheep for reconciliation. And do you know what their most frequent request is? *"Ichaka nying' "* (Name a baby after me).

The intertwining of the life of a baby and an ancestor is so real that if a baby becomes critically ill, the parents take it back to the elder who divined the name of the ancestor that was reborn through the child. They do this on the supposition that perhaps the name was wrong, and that the unnamed living ancestor was causing the sickness to show its displeasure. The elder holds the crying baby and begins to recite the names of the ancestors until the baby stops crying. The name being recited when the baby calms down is seen to be the real ancestral name of the baby. Usually the baby gets well after this ritual.

We see ourselves, Padri, as intimately linked to the ancestors psychologically, emotionally, religiously, and physically through that common life force. That is why we include the unborn along with the ancestors as living members of the human community. In this view the human community encompasses the whole of human life whether ancestral, contemporary, or potential.

At the same time, Mzee Padri, I find your isolation of the dead ancestors to be unreal. Those very people who nurtured you when you were a helpless infant are now seen to be permanently separated from you and to have no real social role or meaning in the land of the living. You seem to be saying that you go on living almost as if they never existed. Yet it is their lives that you share. How can you remove them from your present and future existence?

As Riana finished talking, another group of mourners arrived, wailing and crying as they walked over to the grave to pay their final respects. The Christians among them made the sign of the cross and begin to pray for the deceased person. The conversations of the other people in the homestead seemed to die out as the Christians broke into song: "Jesus, come and live with us forever. Satan, get behind us forever. Jesus, come and live with us forever." One of the Christian women prayed in a loud voice: "Our Father, you have taken our brother. Watch over him well. May he live in peace with you and the ancestors. All these things we ask in the name of Jesus the Lord." Then all said the prayer: "Our Father." A blessing of holy water was sprinkled on the grave, followed by a final sign of the cross. As the group began to disperse, I turned to Riana to answer his question.

MISSIONARY: Riana, my friend, we also dream at night of our ancestors. However, we give dreams an entirely different meaning. We do not feel that these meetings with ancestors while we are sleeping are at all real. They are merely tricks of the mind and imagination. But I can appreciate your interpretation. Maybe we can talk about dreaming at some other time. However, I have been thinking about why we quickly forget the dead. I think it has something to do with our idea that there are two worlds in the cosmos: this broken world of suffering and death experienced by the living and the "other" world of God and the ancestors. Therefore, those who have died are no longer part of this world. As such, we Western Christians have to keep reminding ourselves that God is indeed also present to this imperfect world, this world of pain and tears. However, God's real place is in that other world where the just person finds fulfillment and the evil person eternal frustration. This mentality makes it easy to forget the dead. Besides, those who are saved are in peace and at rest with God. The cares and tribulations of this world have passed away for them. So why should they be concerned with the situation of the living? Moreover, there is no physical evidence that the dead are present to the living, even though our church has officially declared some of the dead to be saints and capable of helping the living. They are said to form a community together with all the saved. However, many of these special saints are described as such exceptional people that it is easy to separate them from the ordinary dead ancestors. They are like special messengers from God to the living, but they are also located in that other world. As a result, we generally think of humanity as embracing only the presently living people. This dualistic split in our teaching is, I think, at the root of our feelings and attitudes toward the dead.

One time I was asked by a group of Pentecostal Christians whether or not the communion of saints is as active in helping the living as the communion of the devil and the damned is in tempting the living. I answered that I supposed it was, although we Christians generally approach the saints on an individual basis. The devil, by way of contrast, is pictured in the popular imagination as a hoard of dangerous spirits prowling about like lions seeking whomever they may devour. The devil is seen to be much more immediate to this world in its power of destruction than the saints in their power to help.

At the same time, Riana, I find your teachings about the unity of the human family, both the living and the dead, to be very attractive. However, if you have such a close relationship with your ancestors, who are the source of your life, why do they not protect you from death? Or, when you die, why don't you accept it as the will of the ancestor, the way we accept death as the will of God? Your ritual of driving death out of the village seems to say that death itself is a sign of some immorality that is threatening the human community and must be neutralized. Is death an event that even the ancestors cannot overcome? Is death always a sign of immorality?

RIANA: Padri, as I have said, nothing happens in human life that is not caused by someone. Therefore, even death has its personal cause. It is important, therefore, that this personal cause be identified in order that others within the homestead or in the community not be struck down. This is why the warriors dress up for battle and drive away the source of death from the village whether it be an evil spirit, a witch, or a charm. Death is driven away by the warriors and the cattle into a desolate place where it is cursed and isolated. By this ritual, all are confident that death is gone. This ritual tells us that death is not a natural thing. It also seems to say that the ancestors are unable to control it once it has been set into motion by immorality. Their saving help is to neutralize it so that it doesn't happen again.

This brings up the point that we touched upon when we talked about evil, namely, that once evil is set loose, it wreaks havoc until it is stopped or neutralized by a stronger power. In this way punishment for evil is immediate; it is not delayed or put off to some future time. The ancestors, because they do not control the source of evil, can only react to evil already set loose, for example, that which has caused the death. There is a distinction, though, between an untimely death and death at an old age. The former is definitely a manifestation of evil at work, the latter is not so clear. Everybody does die and our elderhood rituals seem to prepare a person to meet the ancestors through death—an inevitable event. Consequently, in the death of an old person, there does not seem to be the anxiety about the presence of evil that is felt at an untimely death. It is easier to accept the death of an older person. Maybe the forces of immorality are weaker and not so obvious in those cases. At times, death is even seen as a release for an old person who has suffered for many years.

The questions you are asking, Padri, do not have a simple answer. It is like your belief that at some point in the future all the dead will rise from the grave with their bodies. But how can these bodies be brought back together? What about the people who have drowned at sea and whose bodies were never recovered? What about those who were eaten by wild animals? Even those who are buried—all that is left of their bodies after a few years are the bones. How can these bodies live again? The human evidence is such that the resurrection of the body seems impossible. When you die your body returns to the earth and disappears into dirt. The Christian belief that their bodies will be resurrected seems to be unreal. It is indeed an attractive idea, but it seems to be merely a dream-wish with no possibility of fulfillment.

MISSIONARY: Riana, you are right, the resurrection of the body cannot be proved. But it is a deep-seated belief of the Christian people. After the death of Jesus on a cross, he appeared to his disciples and ate with them. Jesus challenged one of his followers, Thomas, to put his fingers into the wounds in his hands where the nails had been driven when he was hanging on a cross to die. He also invited Thomas to put his hand in the wound in his side where a Roman soldier had speared him with a lance. This Jesus did in order to prove to Thomas that he had really risen from the dead and was still a human being with a body. However, it was clear from the beginning that this resurrected body was very different. Jesus was able to appear in a room without opening the door. He was able to sit at table eating and talking with his disciples without their recognizing him. He could disappear at will. After forty days he went with some of his disciples to the top of a hill and, after commanding them to preach his Good News of salvation to the ends of the earth, he went up into the sky.

From these events the Christian church has always affirmed that the final state of a person will be a human state. That is, a person will not be just a spirit but will be an integrated human person of body and soul. The only model we have for this is what was written about Jesus' body, called a glorified body, in his appearances to his disciples after his resurrection. What the bodies of the damned will be like we have no revelation.

Whether or not the new body will be made up of exactly the same matter as the old body is a question of speculation. Scientifically such a proposition does not seem reasonable, especially since the human body is not a static reality but is changing its shape, its composition, and its chemicals throughout its life. Which state of the body will be preserved and resurrected? The question seems irrelevant. The important element is that we believe that our great creator, God, has the power to give each and every human being a resurrected body of the kind that was given to Jesus. This doctrine is at the heart of our Christian faith. St. Paul, one of our earliest teachers and leaders, wrote that if there is no resurrection from the dead, then he would be among the world's greatest fools.

Another thing, Riana, we also believe that both the good and the evil persons will be resurrected—the former will experience fulfillment, the latter everlasting suffering. What do you believe about the final state of those who die in their evil, people like witches, thieves, and murderers? Are there any eternal sanctions that separate the evil ancestors from the good ones? Are there two communities of ancestors, or are all the dead treated alike? Is retribution for evil found only in this life or does it follow one into the afterlife? Is there a judgment of the great Kiteme on the moral life of a person at death?

RIANA: Well, Mzee, it is hard to answer that question with any certainty. It seems that the ancestors are all together after death, although some do distinguish between the Wahenga, those recently deceased, and the Mahoka, those no longer known. Now, whether or not the evil persons are with the Mahoka is not clear. We do believe, however, that any evil that a person commits in this life has immediate consequences that cannot be avoided. One is always punished *in this life* for the evil that one does. Therefore, when someone dies, he or she is buried without reference to the evil that the person might have done.

I recall the case of a man who was known as a witch by the whole community. When he died, he was buried like anyone else, and his family continues to deny that he was a witch. In the case of a man being beaten to death while stealing, or practicing witchcraft, we have no knowledge. We just assume that all evil is punished and rectified in this life. There is no idea that at death a person is judged on the basis of earlier good or bad deeds—the judgment takes place when the deeds are committed. This is why ordinary people, as I have already explained, when confronted with some serious problem in their lives, immediately begin to wonder if the problem is a punishment for some evil action that they have done or in which they have been involved. It is this anxiety that leads them to consult a diviner to find the source of the evil.

Padri, unfortunately I shall have to end the discussion on this note. It is getting late and the sun is starting to set. I must be getting home. I do not like to travel after dark. There are too many robbers these days with guns, and it is just not worth the risk. Again, I've enjoyed the conversation very much, and I have learned a lot of new things. We definitely have to keep these conversations going. I am now much more sympathetic to the Christian religion. I realize that you Christians are struggling, as much as we are, with these same basic questions about the meaning of life.

MISSIONARY: Riana, this has been a good discussion. Unfortunately, I shall be leaving for the United States next week on a three-month leave, and I do not know whether I shall return to this mission station. If I do not see you before then, I want to thank you again for your friendship and honesty. This has been a good way to create mutual understanding and respect for our religions. However, I doubt if any other Christian leaders would be interested in debating these issues with you. But I shall ask around to see if there is anyone who would like to meet you.

At this point another group of mourners entered into the homestead, wailing loudly and shouting out the name of the deceased. Riana stood up and shook my hand and the hands of several of the elders who had been sitting around listening. I said: "Go with good luck, Riana, and greet everyone for me in the village." Riana responded: "You also go with good luck, and may the ancestors watch over you on the way."

Riana walked off together with a dozen people from his village. The women were carrying their empty food containers on their heads. Several had babies strapped on their backs. Their walk was brisk and purposeful. It would be after dark before they would reach their village ten miles away.

In the homestead of the deceased, a memorial log was smoldering near the grave. This log would be kept burning until the official end of the funeral on the seventh day. At that time the property of the deceased would be divided among his heirs, and his wives would be taken in by his brothers.

As I walked slowly toward my home with a group of people, cattle from the neighboring homesteads were being shepherded back to their corrals for the night. There was the sweet smell of manure in the damp evening air.

COMMENTARY

In this fifth and final chapter, we again see how one's worldview determines the way in which final salvation is understood. For Riana, since there has been no moral separation of humankind and God, salvation must be in terms of the here and now. He thinks of "everlasting life" in terms of the possibility of somehow returning through reincarnation to this world as a human being. It is in this context that the whole scenario of the grandchildren being the returned spirits of the ancestors makes sense. Life for Riana is a continuum embracing the dead, the unborn, and the living. This belief promotes the solidarity of the living and the dead in a way unheard of in Western thought. I am now wondering if Christian salvation can be adequately expressed in terms of a cyclic view of reality. Such a view would certainly revive our concern for and relationship with the dead.

Indeed, where is the Christian community that remembers the past sufferings and trials of our dead Christian brothers and sisters? The answer, of course, is the African Christian community. It continues to remember and relate to the dead, since it perceives the dead as part of the human community—something that is not immediate to Western Christians.

As a Christian missionary with a dipolar worldview, I look elsewhere for an answer to the question of final salvation—the eternal world of God, the saints, and the damned. I also insist that the Christian afterlife, at least for the saved, is a human life because there will be a resurrection of the body. One will not remain a disembodied spirit, as seems to be the case in Riana's belief.

Both Riana and I demand faith in what we believe is the final situation of humanity. Death itself is so silent and final that there is no concrete evidence for either personal resurrection or nominal reincarnation. However, if one sees in the faces and lives of one's children the images and lives of the ancestors, then Riana seems to have the more plausible belief, and the Christian belief in the resurrection of the body is seen to be more extraordinary.

The distinctiveness of particular funeral customs is clear. The Western customs of embalming and concrete boxes, seen as bizarre by Riana, are matched by the "driving out of death rituals" of the Africans, which I found bizarre. Death in all cultures is such a traumatic experience that it usually calls forth certain customs, seen as strange by the outsider, that people do instinctively without realizing the underlying significance.

On the question of eternal sanctions, Riana looks for the resolution of evil in the here and now. There is no transcendent world where the innocent are justified and the guilty are judged. Responsibility for actions is such that the lineal family, and even the clan, shares in the punishment resulting from the sins of one of its members. I, on the other hand, when faced with the insoluble problem of the prosperity of the wicked, am willing to put off the final accounting for one's actions to another time and place—the final judgment. This Christian belief can easily lead one to shirk full responsibility for moral evil in this world, in the belief that justice will be done elsewhere. However, more and more Western Christian theologians with a justice-and-peace perspective are adopting an African-style unitary approach to evil, saying that moral evil must be confronted, struggled against, and neutralized in this world for the sake of the kingdom of God no matter what the cost.

Given Riana's preoccupation with the ancestors and their role in salvation, a fully developed African Christian theology will be very explicit and rich in its teachings about the life and reality of the ancestors. Such a theology will have a great deal to teach the Western Christian church about relationships with the communion of the saints.

The concept of nominal reincarnation is most difficult to pin down and to understand. This is one of those concepts that just does not fit into any ready-made category and must be studied carefully and intensively. I have heard it argued that this reincarnation of the ancestor is like the reincarnation of Christ in each and every Christian. It has also been suggested that the relationship between the ancestor and the infant is like the relationship that is said to exist in the Trinity, among the Father, Son, and Holy Spirit. Likewise I have seen it written that reincarnation of ancestors is understandable because the soul of a person is multifaceted in African thought; there are a variety of spiritual principles that coalesce to form a unique individual. Thus a person is the ancestor from one dimension and his or her own personal self from another.

Both Riana and I are in agreement that there is a life after death. Neither of us questioned this belief. Hence the African people could hear and understand what the Christians were teaching about life after death because they already had a similar belief. Christianity added to and expanded that belief with the ideas of personal immortality and the resurrection of the body—teachings that new converts to Christianity find most attractive. This is another example of how Christianity is always interpreted by the newly evangelized in terms of existing traditional beliefs. Without an understanding of this dialectic process, there will never be an Africanization of Christianity or the creation of an African Christian church self-designed on the level of culture. Furthermore, to the great detriment of the Christian churches, the neocolonialistic Christianization of Africa will continue, unchallenged by even its own indigenous sons and daughters.

The position taken in this book is that this mutual cosmological filtering of the Christian message, with all that this implies theologically, is part and parcel of the normal process of evangelization. Moreover, this process, if it is not blocked, leads in due time to new syntheses combining the best and most authentic elements of both African and Christian theologies. In these syntheses the local Christian theologies of the missionaries are enriched with an African perspective, and the indigenous African theologies begin to take on a Christian perspective—the genesis of indigenous African Christian theologies.

It is not too late to begin the Africanization of Christianity. It may be too late if it is delayed until the coming generation.

Index

Compiled by William E. Jerman

132